"Just like our houses, our work is filled with clutter that's keeping us from what matters most. *Start Finishing* shows us how to pick the ideas and projects that we want to keep and work through seeing them to completion. If you're ready to get over the clutter of busywork and do the work that'll make you come alive, get this book and start finishing."

JOSHUA BECKER
founder of Becoming Minimalist
and author of *The Minimalist Home*

"Big dreams can feel overwhelming, but in this encouraging book, Charlie shows you how to get started, plan your projects, and just keep going. You don't find the time, you *make* the time—and Charlie will show you how."

LAURA VANDERKAM
bestselling author of *Off the Clock: Feel Less Busy While Getting More Done* and *Juliet's School of Possibilities*

"If you're wondering what you should do with your life, Charlie has the answer: start finishing your best work. He goes deep into the real challenges that get in the way when you start making things that matter and teaches you proven, adaptable tools to close the gap between you and the person you want to be. Get this book and figure out your purpose, one finished project at a time."

JEFF GOINS
bestselling author of
Real Artists Don't Starve

"My decades of helping people create their body of work and start businesses have repeatedly shown that the greatest threat to success is the lack of ability to get things done and out into the world. Charlie Gilkey is uniquely qualified to solve this problem, and *Start Finishing* will fundamentally change the creative and entrepreneurial landscapes. Read this book and reap the rewards for the rest of your life."

PAMELA SLIM
author of *Escape from Cubicle
Nation* and *Body of Work*

"Paths are made by walking, not waiting. In *Start Finishing*, Charlie Gilkey lifts us back up and walks us to the finish line of the important goals and ideas we've been sitting on. The result of this book is quite honestly a life filled with fewer distractions and a greater sense of daily fulfillment. It's a must-read that we will undoubtedly be referencing and re-reading in the weeks and months ahead."

MARC AND ANGEL CHERNOFF
New York Times bestselling authors
of *Getting Back to Happy*

"*Start Finishing* offers a step-by-step process to help you get from concept to completed, no matter the project you're trying to tackle. So many books show you how to get going on projects but few focus on how to get beyond the beginning, through the middle, and to the end result. Charlie Gilkey has written a book that does that—and does it in a way that's tried, tested, and true. *Start Finishing* is a book that, once read from start to finish, will allow you finish anything time and time again."

MIKE VARDY
productivity strategist and
founder of TimeCrafting

START
FINISHING

START FINISHING

HOW TO GO FROM IDEA TO DONE

CHARLIE GILKEY

sounds true
BOULDER, COLORADO

Sounds True
Boulder, CO 80306

Published 2019

Cover design by Rachael Murray
Book design by Beth Skelley
Illustrations © 2019 Productive Flourishings

Printed in South Korea

Library of Congress Cataloging-in-Publication Data

Names: Gilkey, Charlie, author.
Title: Start finishing : how to go from idea to done / Charlie Gilkey.
Description: Boulder, CO : Sounds True, [2019]
Identifiers: LCCN 2018059665 (print) | LCCN 2019011121 (ebook) |
    ISBN 9781683643241 (ebook) | ISBN 9781683642633 (hardcover)
Subjects: LCSH: Time management. | Procrastination.
Classification: LCC HD69.T54 (ebook) | LCC HD69.T54 G55 2019 (print) |
    DDC 658.4/04—dc23
LC record available at https://lccn.loc.gov/2018059665

10 9 8 7 6 5 4 3 2 1

For Mom, who placed so many people's thriving above her own, and Dad, who in another place and time would've stunned the world with what he finished.

It is always about the work. In the latter years of your life, your happiness and your self-esteem will be determined by the mountains you surmounted, the valleys you climbed out of, and the life and/ or career that you forged for yourself.

MAYA ANGELOU, *Rainbow in the Cloud*

CONTENTS

PART 1

CLEARING THE DECKS
FOR YOUR BEST WORK

The work of today is the history of
tomorrow, and we are its makers.
JULIETTE GORDON LOW,
How Girls Can Help Their Country

"SOMEDAY" CAN BE TODAY

Take a moment and think about the last two weeks of your
life. How much of your time and attention has been focused
on things that truly matter to you?

Most people's honest answer is, "Not enough."

Buried under busywork, responsibility, distraction, and
fatigue sit the difference-making and joy-producing ideas,
waiting for someday . . .

when the time's right,

when this project's over,

when you have a little more money,

when the kids are grown,

when you get a more understanding boss,

or . . . someday.

The trouble is "someday" never comes on its own.

My goal with this book is to get you to decide that today
is the day you stop waiting and start finishing.

The reason I'm guiding you to finish rather than start is
because I'm near certain that you've already started quite a
few things. Somewhere along the way, in physical, mental,
and digital drawers, those brilliant ideas are waiting on the

someday that you'll get back to them and figure out what actually needs to happen to get the ideas out into the world.

Starting only stuffs more stuff into those already-full drawers. Enough is enough.

YOU KNOW YOU'RE NOT WORKING ON WHAT MATTERS MOST

It would be extremely presumptive for me to claim you have some unfinished important projects were it not for the fact that I've yet to find a person who hasn't had an idea or project that they've hidden away. Even the extremely successful professionals I've interviewed and run with admit that there's something calling to them that they're not getting to.

It would be one thing if you didn't know you weren't working on what matters most, for we all often get distracted and trapped under busywork. But there's a part of you that knows it's there and won't let it go. That part sees a world above the noise, ephemera, and getting by—and it sees a path to get there.

Unfortunately that path is just a formless idea. We don't do ideas; we do projects.

By *project* I mean anything that takes time, energy, and attention to complete. There's no difference between a work project or a personal project when it comes to pulling from the limited time, energy, and attention we have. The difference comes in the way we prioritize work and personal projects, with the former given more weight because they're much more tied to our livelihood, status, and identities than the latter.

Just to be clear . . .

Figuring out what your kids need to go back to school is a project.

Getting married (or divorced) is a project.

Organizing the Closet of Doom is a project.

Looking for a new job is a project.

Volunteering for the bake sale at church is a project.

Going on a new diet is a project.

Finding a new drummer because you just can't deal with Steve flaking on you anymore is a project.

Starting a new business of any size is a project.

Moving to a different house or apartment is a project.

I'm belaboring the point here because those kinds of projects too often aren't counted as projects, but they use time, energy, and attention. Many people end up with their days filled with projects they aren't counting, but what does count to them are counted projects that aren't getting done.

To get to the place our soul longs to be, we're going to have to convert our ideas into doable projects at the same time that we're going to have to get real about all the projects we *are* doing. The problem isn't that we're lazy or incapable—it's just that we're not doing the work that's going to enable us to thrive.

WE THRIVE BY DOING OUR BEST WORK

Sages from Aristotle to the Dalai Lama have asserted that the goal of human action is to thrive. Language, cultural context, and nuance vary, but the rough idea is the same.

Switching the emphasis from "thrive" to "human action" reveals one of the surprising double meanings that wisdom maxims usually carry: we thrive via action, or, more simply stated, we thrive by doing.

The obvious challenge is that there are certain kinds of actions that lead to our thriving, or else the mindless clicking we too easily succumb to would be filling our thrive-o-meter. Luckily, you already know the doing you need to do to move you toward thriving. Yes, it's tied to the idea that's nagging you.

I call the work that leads to our thriving *best work*, but because work is a complex concept that comes with a variety of meanings, contexts, and connotations—many of which are negative—I'll describe what I'm calling best work.

YOUR BEST WORK CAN BE SACRED

An oddity of the English language is that so many expletives and profane words are four letters long. These words describe things we want to avoid doing or talking about, or at the very least they're words we don't use in polite company. In many contexts, *work* has fallen into the same emotional buckets those words are in: we don't want to do it, we don't want to talk about it, and we do as little of it as possible.

But *work* isn't necessarily a four-letter word in that sense. It can be sacred. It can be what makes us come alive. It can be joyful. It can be something we're so inspired to do that it almost feels wrong to get paid to do it. It can be what makes us eager to end our vacation so we can get back to doing it, not because we're overwhelmed by being behind but rather it's something we feel like we *get* to do rather than *have* to do. This kind of work is our best work.

ONLY YOU CAN DO YOUR BEST WORK

Whatever your best work is, it's something that *only you* can do. Only you have the set of experiences, expertise, skills, and perspectives to do it. In this great orchestra of creation of which we're all a part, no one can play your instrument the way you do.

This means that if you don't do your best work, we miss out. The unique creations, outcomes, relationships, or conditions that result from your best work can't be replaced or re-created by anyone else. There may be close copies, but much like how minuscule differences in our DNA create remarkably different people, a close copy of your best work will be remarkably different than what you would create.

YOUR BEST WORK SERVES YOU *AND* OTHERS

Doing your best work neither requires you to selfishly do whatever you most want to do nor to be a lifelong martyr in service to other people's needs. It's as if we all have some kind of tree that we're somehow wired to enjoy planting. Your best work uniquely serves you by planting that tree and by the fruit it yields while simultaneously serving others by your doing so.

Countless interviews with people doing their best work bear out this strange phenomenon. Whether it's soldiers who couldn't imagine being anything else, nonprofit leaders who have dedicated years to advancing their causes, artists who are continually surprised that the work they love to create benefits others, or business leaders who wake up in the morning creating organizations worth being a part of, in each case there's no either/or perspective about who's being served by the work they're doing. It's *all*.

YOUR BEST WORK REQUIRES *REALLY* SHOWING UP

But just because your best work is uniquely yours to do and you're served by doing it doesn't mean that it's somehow easy to do. In fact, that it's your best work can often mean that it's harder to do, for several reasons.

First, it's harder to do because how you do it will be different. Learning from books and others can get you started, but at a certain point you'll have to start blazing your own trail and end up in the no-man's-land where everyone doing their best work ends up. Braving this uncertainty and making it up as you go along isn't for the faint of heart.

Second, if you're doing your best work, you'll always be on the edge of your capabilities and comfort levels. Imagine a Venn diagram, with your current capabilities in the left circle and your areas of incompetence in the right circle. Learning and growth happens right where those two intersect. Doing your best work will thus require you to constantly be on the verge of failing.

Third, your best work, because it serves others, will have a public-facing component. Some people you share it with will love it and expect you to do more of it. Others will hate it. Some people will be meh about it and want you to take it in a different direction. You'll be in the center of a storm of other people's opinions and have to remain able to endure it and walk forward nonetheless.

It's thus no wonder why so many people aren't doing their best work. Sticking to the known and safe path doesn't require nearly as much courage, discipline, and vision.

YOUR BEST WORK IS EASILY DISPLACED BY OTHER STUFF

Since doing your best work requires really showing up for extended periods of time, it's easy to displace it with other stuff. There's always something to do that's easier, more urgent, more understandable, less risky, or more likely to please others. There's always some idyllic time in the future when it will make sense to focus on your best work.

A life can easily be spent "in the meantime," between now and that idyllic time when you're able to do your best work. In that meantime, rocking your to-do lists displaces doing your best work. Thriving in your life is more than just getting things done if the things getting done aren't your best work.

YOUR BEST WORK IS MORE THAN JUST YOUR "JOB"

Your best work may not be translatable to work you would do in a conventional day job. It could be raising your kids. It could be a side business or starting a full-time business. It could be working with a nonprofit, unpaid, or in part-time government service; volunteering at your church, coaching Little League, or mentoring teenagers. It could be a hobby.

It's sometimes useful to figure out how you can make a living by doing your best work, but your best work may not lend itself to being an economic engine. This doesn't make it any less meaningful, valuable, or important, for not everything that's meaningful, valuable, or important is tradable in the marketplace or will be "bought" enough to create a living for yourself.

The primary consideration is thus not how your best work will support your livelihood but how your best work fits into a meaningful life for you.

It may be that you can only do ten hours a week of your best work, but even people whose best work creates a living for them may only get to do ten hours a week of their best work. You may also create different options for yourself, such as deliberately working part time and earning less so you can do more of your best work or collaborating with your partner so that you have more weekend time to devote to your best work.

The grace is that your best work *doesn't* have to be your full-time job. The downside is that not having it as your full-time job removes a lot of excuses and justifications for not doing it.

WE LIVE IN A PROJECT WORLD

To move from the aspiration of thriving to doing our best work, we're going to need to convert our ideas that matter into projects that find a place on our schedule. I call these kinds of projects *best-work projects* to demarcate them from all the other projects we may be doing or thinking about doing.

The way I'm using *project* has a major trade-off: we trade clarity for potential overwhelm, for we better see that *everything* is a project at the same time that there's a lot of them and they come in different sizes. I think it's a trade-off worth making, though, because it allows us to reexamine our lives and careers.

Take our professional careers. Rather than thinking of our best work as contained by a decades-long stretch working at one company, we can think about it as it truly is: a series of major projects that each last three to five years and contain a lot of other smaller projects. Your current position at your company is a three- to five-year project that will propel you into another. If you're in school right now, each level of education is a leg of a three- to five-year journey. And if you're running a business, in three to five years, your role in the business—and what your business is—will change, and that's the point.

Our lives follow a similar pattern. Every three to five years something is importantly different. We move to new places. Our kids, siblings, and parents go through thresholds that may require us to adapt. We go through stages of dating and marriage every three to five years. Over the course of three to five years we age and aren't able to do some things like we used to, but we find other things to do.

When we take this higher view, we see that we're simultaneously chaotic and remarkably consistent beings. Like clockwork, our inner and outer worlds are going to change every three to five years. *What* the change will be, we're not sure, but we know that there *will* be change.

Since we live in this project world, we can embrace the uncertainty of it while simultaneously being intentional about what projects we're doing. The grace of this project world is that we don't have to collapse into analysis paralysis and think we're making nonreversible long-term decisions when it comes to picking our projects. If we pick the "wrong" project, we'll switch to another one once we see it through. If we pick the "right" project, we'll switch to another one once we see it through.

And when it comes to our long-term best-work projects, we often can't see where the projects are going to take us in advance; we'll be creating new realities and possibilities that we simply can't see because they don't presently exist. Think about something you've done that really mattered to you and how many things unfolded that you never saw coming. Your best-work projects follow the twentieth-century Spanish poet Antonio Machado's maxim, "Wanderer, there is no road, the road is made by walking."

PROJECTS ARE MIRRORS AND BRIDGES

Throughout this book I'll be guiding you to convert an idea into a doable project that you drive to the finish line. While it's always great to finish a best-work project, the reason we're taking this approach is because I've found that projects are both mirrors of what's going on in our current world and bridges to a better world.

Projects are mirrors because they reflect back to us what's really going on in our inner and outer worlds. Showing some specific piece of work to the world shows *us* where our passions and fears lie. Being naturally excited enough to get up early or stay up late to work on some specific project shows us as much as dreading going to bed on Sunday night because we don't want the workweek to begin. Doing a best-work project will require us to show up when it gets challenging. At the same time, that best-work project itself will create more challenges than normal, but the project itself is just a mirror for what's going on with us and the world.

Projects are bridges because it's only by doing them that we create the paths our souls want to walk. As we create and change the world, we create and change ourselves. But we don't do real creation and change work in our heads; we have to roll up our sleeves and mix the stuff of the world together to create new realities.

So throughout this book I will continually prompt you to return to a specific idea that you'll turn into a project and finish because it's the single best way to really see how the insights of the book reflect your world and to build a bridge to the world you want to create. You may be surprised at what you scc and build if you actually roll up your sleeves and start finishing your best-work project.

EMBRACE YOUR "SCATTERED" BEST WORK

Some people are blessed to have a narrow set of interests that seem to endlessly fascinate them, but there are a lot of us Renaissance souls who have a hard time fitting into one easy label. People like us start getting suspicious when people tell us to pick one project because too often we're forced to choose to present one shade of our multihued self to others and then we're identified by that shade.

We're not just a writer. We're a writer *and* a drone engineer.

We're not just a product distribution manager. We're a product distribution manager *and* a community activist.

We're not just a pastor. We're a pastor *and* a derby girl.

Actually, we probably have quite a few *ands*, and, to us, those *ands* aren't flavor text—they're the core of who we are.

I want you to embrace those *ands*. At the same time, I'm going to reinforce what you already know: each of those *ands* requires upkeep in terms of projects. We'll cover some ways you can weave those different projects together later in the book, but I want to let you know from the beginning that you're not going to have to choose *one* way to be in the world or *one* domain for your best work.

HOW A PHILOSOPHER-SOLDIER TURNS INTO A PRODUCTIVITY TEACHER

I get the whole "my best work is all over the place" thing because it's a pretty good summary of my life too.

In 2004, I was twenty-four years old and a year into my graduate studies in philosophy when my Army National Guard unit deployed in support of Operation Iraqi Freedom. I was a lieutenant at the time, and my job was to ensure my forty-five soldiers delivered equipment throughout the bomb-laden roads in Iraq. I was out with them on the convoys as well, which led to me balancing my personnel management responsibility with tactical convoy command duties.

Midway through the deployment, I was pulled into higher headquarters to be the battalion plans officer, where my chief responsibility was to write or review the plans for every convoy movement in the battalion, which happened to be one of the most active and efficient transportation battalions in the theater. Later on, two important additional duties were added to my plate: monitoring and supporting our convoys in real time and doing the after-action reviews (AARs) for convoys that were ambushed, had accidents, or otherwise went unexpectedly off course. During these AARs, my job was to figure out what happened, why it happened, how the troops responded, and what effects their response had, all in the effort to create or update our tactics, techniques, and procedures across the battalion (and theater) so that we got better at accomplishing the mission and bringing more healthy soldiers home.

Two weeks after my unit came home, I was back in classes and ready to get back to my life. But the crucible that was that year changed me—for the better. Esoteric conversations on epistemology and metaphysics no longer held my interest, not because I didn't understand what was going on but because they seemed detached from the real problems we face individually, culturally, and globally. I dove deeper into ethics, human rights, and social and political philosophy, as ever more my interests were on what it means to thrive, be good people, and build the communities, societies, and institutions that lead to thriving.

As my dual careers as an officer and scholar progressed, I was vexed by the fact that, though I could plan, coordinate, and lead hundreds of troops and trucks, I was challenged as a scholar by a few papers a semester. I (almost) always finished them on time and did well, but it felt more like barely managed chaos than what I thought it should. So I did what both my professions had trained me to do: I started researching the solutions other people had created to address my challenges.

Most of what I read didn't hit the target, though. The personal productivity literature was too nitty-gritty and focused on tasks, and the personal development literature focused on principles and big ideas. But my problem was in the messy middle where creative projects live. After a few years of reading, applying, retranslating, and toolmaking for myself, I did what both my professions had taught me to do: I started sharing my insights, retranslations, syntheses, and tools with other people at what would become my website, Productive Flourishing.

THE JOURNEY TO FINISHING

This book is organized into three distinct parts that roughly track what you'll need to do to go from idea to done. Here in part 1, "Clearing the Decks for Your Best Work," we'll cover the general landscape of the world we work in and the inner landscape that's inside all of us and get clear on what matters to us. In part 2, "Planning Your Project," we'll discuss how to make space for your project and how to convert it into a working project plan and explore some common obstacles that get in the way once you make that plan. In part 3, "Working the Plan," we'll work through how to get that road map on your schedule and work through the ups, downs, and sideways that happen when reality does its annoying habit of not looking like what you thought it would.

I've written the book so that you can jump into any part and still get something out of it, but there are three ways you can read this book:

1 **From start to finish.** If the idea of doing more of your best work feels unrealistic, reading the book from start to finish is the best route because the book addresses root-cause challenges as it goes along. Your project will be a great mirror and bridge for you, but you'll build in some reaction, reflection, and journaling time too.

2 **As a way of working through a stage of a project.** Part 2 is heavily project focused, so jump in there.

3 **To get ideas on how to solve a specific problem.** Chapters 7, 8, and 9 are particularly helpful because they address common challenges that happen at the weekly and daily levels.

My goal isn't to be the definitive and complete voice on all the topics in this book but rather to present a distilled version of the insights, strategies, and practices that I've incorporated from my decades of training, research, practice, and experimentation. A lot of my work is naming the roadblocks, patterns, mindsets, and practices that support and get in the way of our ability to do our best work, for naming them makes it easier to spot what's going on and to know what to do in response.

Books on productivity, creativity, and personal development often oddly tend to make people feel bad about themselves. So I want to be clear up front: you aren't uniquely defective, you aren't constitutionally wired to struggle, and you aren't fated to be unable to get your shit together. If I point out the ridiculous, absurd, and self-defeating ways we think and act, it's so I can lay bare the lies so we can see them for what they truly are. We're more than the thoughts we have and actions we take, and we can adopt new thoughts and take new actions that lead us to be the best versions of ourselves. And throughout this book, I use *we* as often as *you* because we—including myself—have common struggles and patterns, even when we think we've transcended those struggles and patterns.

You're more than you think you are because we're *all* more than we think we are. You can rewrite the stories that keep you from being your best self. You can change the way you show up, how you plan, and how you respond when things inevitably get tough. You can be successful without burning out or being a hermit.

(Yes, you!)

I will be relentless about there being more potential in you than we can ever know. It's the only truth I know that explains how teenagers fresh out of high school become heroes on the battlefield, depressed introverts become creative leaders in their fields, or unassuming soccer moms start nonprofits that change their lives, their families' lives, and their communities. I've been in the arena with them and have witnessed these changes happening—sometimes slowly, sometimes quickly. The only thing that's unique about the people who stand up and move forward is that they stand up and move forward.

I don't know how you got here, and none of us know where your road will lead. All we know is that you deserve your best work, and the world will be better off for it too.

I've got your back and believe in you. Let's do this.

CHAPTER 1 TAKEAWAYS

▸ We don't do ideas—we do projects.

▸ A project is anything that requires time, energy, and attention to complete.

▸ We thrive by doing our best work.

▸ Our lives and careers are marked by three- to five-year segments that can be thought of as projects.

▸ Projects are mirrors because they reflect back to us what's really going on in our inner and outer worlds; projects are bridges because it's only by doing them that we create the paths ours souls want to walk.

▸ Every "and" aspect of ourselves requires upkeep in the form of projects.

▸ We can create new realities for ourselves, but only when we let go of the idea that we're uniquely defective.

Nothing splendid has ever been achieved except by those who dared to believe that something inside them was superior to circumstances.
BRUCE BARTON, *The Man Nobody Knows*

GETTING TO YOUR BEST WORK

There's a good chance that you've seen the gap between the work you're currently doing and the best work you're yearning to do. There's also a really good chance that you've tried to start doing more of your best work before. One of the first things you probably encountered is that, after a few hours or days of doing it, the commitments, expectations, and challenges of your normal life rudely disrupted your best intentions and took back over.

If your best work was like everything else you're doing, you could just write it off as something you didn't really want to do. But what makes it your best work is that, deep down, you actually want to do it. And, even more, you *need* to do it and the world needs you to do it. So it's more than just a matter of finding the motivation or drive to do your best work—you have to address the parts of your life that are keeping you from doing it.

We're addressing this gap *before* we pick an idea that matters because, if you're like most people, your ideas will be unconsciously constrained to what you think you can fit into your status quo. Since doing your best work will change your status quo anyway, let's look at what's maintaining it.

THE AIR SANDWICH: WHY YOUR BIG PICTURE AND DAY-TO-DAY REALITY DON'T LINK UP

Imagine your life as if it were two slices of bread. Your vision, mission, purpose, and big goals compose the top slice of bread; your day-to-day reality is the bottom slice of bread. For many people, there's a big gap between the two, leading to an *air sandwich*.[1]

At least that's the way that it seems. In between the two slices of bread are actually five different challenges that combine to keep us from spending our days working on what matters most:

▸ Competing priorities
▸ Head trash
▸ No realistic plan
▸ Too few resources
▸ Poor team alignment

Let's take a look at each of these in turn.

COMPETING PRIORITIES

Herding one goat is pretty straightforward; no matter how squirrelly it is, you can rein it in. Herding seven squirrelly goats is considerably harder because each goat goes its own way in search of whatever's driving it at the moment.

Our lives are much closer to the seven-goat scenario in the sense that we're often pulled in different directions to

---

1. Tara Gentile introduced me to Nilofer Merchant's use of "Air Sandwich" in a business context in 2016. I immediately saw the application for individuals.

fulfill our desires. Our roles as parents require us to do things that may be at odds with our careers. Our desires to exercise seem to be at odds with our other hobbies. Our desires to travel can be at odds with our desires to save money. We have *competing priorities*.

Not every desire becomes a priority, but our deepest desires inform those priorities, especially if we believe Mahatma Gandhi's "action expresses priority." But even after we elevate some desires as priorities, they still compete. They're just bigger, more insistent, and squirrelier goats at that point.

What's even more challenging is that some of our operative priorities aren't even ours or are nearly invisible to us. For instance, we prioritize keeping up with the Joneses unconsciously, and parents will sometimes discount how high a priority raising their children is when they examine why other things aren't happening. So, on the one hand, we're herding goats that don't belong to us, and, on the other hand, we're not counting some of the goats that we should be counting.

HEAD TRASH

In chapter 1, we quickly surveyed some of the stories we tell ourselves. Along with those general aspersions and self-limiting stories, we carry our own individual *head trash* that's based on our own personal experiences, histories, and contexts.

While it's true that much of this head trash is formed from our childhood experiences and families of origin, we also pick up new trash as adults. For instance, after a long string of not being able to create plans that work, we may tell ourselves that we're either not good at planning or we're "creative"—that is, not the type of person who can create and follow a plan. Thus when it comes time to do something big that requires planning,

"What else could this mean?" That's a simple question we need to ask ourselves more often. A practical way to apply such a question to our lives is by using a reframing tool we initially picked up from research professor Brené Brown, which we then tailored through our coaching work with students. We call the tool *The story I'm telling myself*. Although asking the question itself—"What else could this mean?"—can help reframe our thoughts and broaden our perspectives, using the phrase "The story I'm telling myself" as a prefix to troubling thoughts can provide an even greater dose of healthy perspective.

Here's how it works: Let's pretend one of your recent goals didn't work out as planned and essentially backfired, and now a few days have passed and you're still feeling upset because you're obviously not capable of achieving anything worthwhile, ever. When you catch yourself feeling this way, use the phrase: The story I'm telling myself is that I was unable to achieve my goal because I'm completely incapable of ever getting worthwhile, positive results in life.

Then ask yourself:

▸ Can I be absolutely certain this story is true? (Is there proof? Is there proof to the contrary?)

▸ What's one other (more constructive) possibility that might also make the ending to this story true?

Give yourself the space to think it through carefully. Challenge yourself to think differently! Use *The story I'm telling myself* to do a reality check with a more constructive mindset.

Marc and Angel Chernoff are *New York Times* bestselling authors of *Getting Back to Happy: Change Your Thoughts, Change Your Reality, and Turn Your Trials into Triumphs* and the creators of *Marc & Angel Hack Life,* which was recognized by *Forbes* as "one of the most popular personal development blogs." Through their writing, coaching, and live events, they've spent the past decade sharing proven strategies for getting unstuck in order to find lasting happiness and success.

we *can't* finish it, and we may end up creating another story about our not being able to do those best-work projects.

Some of us end up creating or holding on to stories that we're somehow uniquely defective. Despite the ample evidence of people who are otherwise like us managing to be successful, overcoming difficulties, and mastering themselves, there's something *about us* such that it won't work for us. We end up fulfilling our own prophecy that we're uniquely defective because other people just like us have figured it out and we haven't.

Head trash *always* looks absurd when you state it directly because you see it for what it is. It's the adult version of the monster under the bed; its power over us rests upon it remaining in the darkness.

NO REALISTIC PLAN

No realistic plan is a loaded challenge, with all three words being incredibly important. Some folks have a plan, but it's not realistic. Others don't have a plan because they don't think it's important or they're not "the planning type." Others confuse an aspiration or idea for a plan and aren't getting anywhere.

To overcome the air sandwich, you're going to need to connect your vision, purpose, and big goals with your day-to-day reality, and the type of projects that do that require creating realistic plans. Much of this book will show you how to do that, as well as how to create plans that adapt and shift with reality.

TOO FEW RESOURCES

Many of us defer our best work because we think we have *too few resources* to achieve our goals. If we had more money, we'd start that nonprofit. If we had more time, we'd write the book. If we had the right contacts, we'd run for office.

In the meantime, we're busy running down roads that may not necessarily get us any closer to the resources we need. And even when those roads serendipitously reveal the resources we need, we often don't see them because we're not open to seeing them in the same way that we don't notice the coffee shop because we're looking for a Starbucks.

President Theodore Roosevelt's[2] "do what you can, with what you've got, where you are" also seems not to apply to us because *our* thing requires a lot more to start than what we have. We thus let what we don't have keep us from creating what we *can* have.

POOR TEAM ALIGNMENT

We normally think about teams in the context of work or sports, but I'm applying teams to the broader cast of characters in your life. Similarly, I'm distinguishing your team from the mere people around you, because a lot of the people around you aren't relevant to your doing your best work.

Think about those times in which you and your partner, friends, coworkers, or community were aligned and focused on shared goals. Now think about the times you weren't. There's likely a *huge* difference in effort, results, and joy between the two.

---

2. Though this quote is a ubiquitous Roosevelt-ism, he attributed it to Squire Bill Widener in his autobiography.

Many of us have *poor team alignment* not because the people on our team are in conflict but because we're not communicating to our team what we want, need, and dream to be.

We may do this because we have the wrong people on our team and we're thus afraid to be vulnerable enough to express our wants, needs, and dreams. In other cases, we do it because we don't actually know what our true wants, needs, and dreams are and we're waiting for inspiration to find us. In the meantime, people are following their own course and we often join their thing at the cost of our own.

THE FIVE CHALLENGES WORK IN CONCERT

We each struggle with one or two of the challenges above more than the others, but we also have *multiple* challenges working on us at once. That's part of the reason we can remain stuck in the grind—we're adept at solving simple, single-pronged challenges; complex, multipronged challenges, not so much.

For instance, because we've "learned" that we're not the planning type (head trash), we have no realistic plan for how to do that big best-work project. Thus we don't realize that there are small ways to get started (too few resources), and those around us who could help, don't (poor team alignment). Or because we're torn between wanting to travel or keeping our kids in a stable school environment (competing priorities), we don't see that we can plan travel trips around school breaks (no realistic plan) and don't save to do it (too few resources).

While "one thing at a time" is *usually* a prudent guideline, it doesn't apply in addressing these five challenges. We *can* work on all of them at once in the sense that by *intentionally* working on one, we can address the others. To take the first example above, as soon as we embrace that there's no such thing as a "planning type" (or that we can be one), we can start to create a realistic plan that uses the resources we have available and ask people to help us. Of course, asking people to help us may trigger more head trash about needing to ask for help, but we're at least one step closer to making our days match the vision of our lives.

THE FIVE KEYS TO OVERCOMING THE AIR SANDWICH

When we have the urge to address the air sandwich, we naturally reach for to-do lists, plans, apps, and books, but that often fails because, at best, those tools address top-level issues. The challenges filling the air sandwich rest a level *below* those issues. For instance, there's nothing intellectually difficult about planning our day; the challenge lies in following that plan, and there's no killer app, system, or big idea that's going to help us do that.

What *will* help us do that is discipline and boundaries. The core keys to unlocking our best work include:

▸ Intention
▸ Awareness
▸ Boundaries
▸ Courage
▸ Discipline

These keys are a modern-day synthesis of Aristotelian virtues and habits. I'm using *virtue* in the same way that Aristotle used it, in the sense that it's a practiced behavior that we can over- or undercultivate. Either cultivation extreme leads to diminished thriving; the goal is to find the middle way between these extremes. The millennia-old challenge of applying the right key in the right amount remains just as challenging as it's always been, but if the air sandwich shows us which doors need to be unlocked, we at least have five keys that can unlock any of those doors.

Let's take a look at each individual key before we start to see how they can be used to address the air sandwich.

INTENTION

Start with *why*. Begin with the end in mind. Consider where you want your life to be in three years. These common phrases all point to the same thing using different language: *intention*.

Most of our conversations about purpose are anchored to intention. The assumption is that if we know our purpose, we'll be more intentional about how we spend our days and life. If we don't know our purpose, then our actions can feel random or meaningless. (So the story goes—a lot of purpose-seeking is deeply rooted and nicely camouflaged fear of uncertainty.)

Intention comes up in nearly every conversation I have with clients and students because we're discussing planning. To make a plan, you have to set a goal. Plans and goals are intentions about the way you will (and won't) use your time, as well as what is and isn't important to you. Many of us don't do our best work because we haven't set a clear intention to do it, especially when we zoom down to how we're planning our days.

Undercultivation of intention is easier to grasp and see in ourselves and others than overcultivation of intention, at least at first blush. But when we look around and see how stricken with anxiety people are because they're so focused on achieving certain goals by certain times by certain ways, it's easy to see how much people's suffering comes from being attached to the world matching their intention. The world has an annoying way of not doing what we want it to, but as the thirteenth-century Persian poet Rumi said, "Yesterday I was clever, so I wanted to change the world. Today I am wise, so I am changing myself."[3]

But for intention to have any grip, it has to be *about something*. One of the chief reasons we're using a project as an anchor for changing our work is because it gives us a focal point to be intentional about how we're specifically using our time, energy, and attention on the project. The project is analogous to focusing on our breath or a specific feeling in meditation.

AWARENESS

"Know thyself" is a cardinal maxim that appears in foundational philosophies from around the world, from Socrates to Lao Tzu to the Buddha to the Bhagavad Gita to the Bible. In each case, calamity comes to those who don't know who they are.

Setting existential considerations aside, we can still see how important *awareness* is. For instance, when we're

---

3. Afzal Iqbal, *The Life and Work of Jalal-ud-din Rumi* (Selangor, Malaysia: Other Press, 2014).

planning to do our best work, we should base our plans on what kind of energy and how much time we have available to us. Deep, creative, and focused work requires a certain kind of energy. Some of us are especially cantankerous or especially friendly at certain times of the day. And so on.

Awareness is required to *know* what your best work is and to notice how your emotions and presence shift when you're doing your best work. A rare few of us seem to know exactly what our best work is, whereas many of us have to pay attention to whispers in our minds and light touches in our hearts to find our way to it. Cultivating the awareness to pay attention to when we're lit up, wondrous, and in flow, or when we're stifled, numb, and full of dread, is critical to growth.

Much of this book thus far has been about creating awareness. Seeing the challenges and opportunities of the project world lets us embrace swimming in the ocean of change rather than being crushed by its waves. Seeing what's filling the air sandwich helps us identify how we might mitigate those challenges. You can neither use nor beat what you can't see.

BOUNDARIES

Most conversations on *boundaries* discuss them in the context of *social* boundaries. Those conversations typically focus on the importance of limiting what behavior you'll accept from others and how you'll respond to create space away from them and those behaviors. While that's important, it's a very limiting view of boundaries that often leads to people not wanting to discuss boundaries; they see them as being about pushing people out or opening the door for them to be pushed away from other people.

We can take a more expansive view of boundaries, though. There are positive and negative boundaries, with positive boundaries creating space *for* something and negative boundaries creating space *from* something. The aforementioned social boundaries are negative boundaries. A positive social boundary would be the space we might create for our kids, partner, or friends. While it's true that we often have to push something away to create space for something—that is, to create a positive boundary, we often have to simultaneously create a negative boundary—it's the intention that matters here. Many people's negative boundaries collapse because they aren't clear what they've made that space for.

If you don't set up boundaries *for* your best work and *from* the things that keep you from doing it, your best work will always be displaced by other things. Setting up and maintaining boundaries can be hard—it's not just you. But like so many things in life, it's worth it.

COURAGE

There's an abundance of smart, compassionate people with ideas worth finishing and ample know-how who can't get momentum on those ideas for the simple reason that their courage is lacking. *Courage* is more important than talent when it comes to finishing what matters most, for courageous action can build talent, but fear keeps us stuck in the confines of yesterday.

I'm aware that *courage* conjures heroic stories such as soldiers in battle, firefighters saving people, or people standing up against machines of injustice. For many people, a courageous action is something that ends up on the news or in books and movies.

While it's true that those *are* acts of courage and should be commended,

typifying larger-than-life heroic actions as courage can too easily mask the everyday courage we need to thrive; it also gives us an easy out.

Every day that you make a choice to do your best work is a day you practice being courageous. Every day that you initiate or participate in a hard conversation or maintain a boundary is a day you practice being courageous. Every day that you dare to share your best work with someone is a day you practice being courageous. Every day that you lean into a "stuck and not getting anywhere" phase of work rather than run from it is a day you practiced courage.

Of course, it's also true that every day you punt that hard conversation, avoid your best work, or run from a stuck project is a day you practice cowardice and make it easier to take the cowardly route the next time. No one wants to be called a coward or wear the mantle; it's within our power to avoid that fate.

When we properly identify lack of courage as what's keeping us from doing our best work and thriving, it allows us to ask more powerful and pointed questions about how to go forward. For instance, when we mistakenly believe we have a knowledge gap, we put research on our action list. But when it comes to our best work, there will always be a chasm between the information we'd like to have and the information we can acquire, for both the inputs and outcomes of our best work are uncertain. Our best work changes us and the world in ways that no present information can fully capture.

In a similar vein, if we think we have a competency or talent gap—which we more often articulate as not being good enough—then it's really easy to spend time in safe learning environments that more often reinforce that we're not good enough than push us to grow in ways that propel our best work forward. Years and scores of thousands of dollars are spent getting degrees and certificates that fundamentally don't cultivate people's courage such that they can thrive in the professional world.

Humor me here. Think about one of your top three most important projects. Ask yourself two questions about the project:

1 What's the smartest next step on this project?

2 What's the most courageous next step on this project?

Your answers to these questions will likely be wildly different if you're being honest with yourself, not just in how you feel about them but also in how you would go about taking that next step. The reality is that your smartest next step is probably the most courageous next step. We don't need more geniuses; we need more courageous people.

If you're doing your best work, you *will* face a continual stream of chances to back down when fear shows its ugly head—and fear is strongest when it *doesn't* show its ugly head and instead lurks, unseen, in the background. Information, know-how, talent, or general readiness will insufficiently arm you to step forward. Courage and the faith it inspires are your only weapons and armor.

Luckily, it's all you need, and the more you use it, the stronger it gets.

DISCIPLINE

That a disciplined person with much less talent and experience can brute-force their way into success inspires no end of frustration for us creatives. While we're quarter-working on the ideas and interests that we absolutely can't let go of, they have advanced their "too narrow," "too specific," "too unoriginal" (by our evaluation) work a few steps forward. In response, we go back to not working even harder during the day and eating more ice cream in the evenings.

At a deep level we know our frustration isn't really about the disciplined folks grinding their way to success but rather our own *discipline*. We know how much more we'd thrive and be happy if we were disciplined. Yet we often feel constitutionally wired to *not* be disciplined, so much so that even the word *discipline* is something that provokes a visceral reaction for many of us. (I suspect that you're only still reading this section because your curiosity and self-awareness has overruled the grimacing and urge to skip on to something more comfortable.)

Our innate talent, creativity, and drive *combined* with discipline are what make us forces of nature.

Without discipline, though, we can be miserable, petty, and unfulfilled. Discipline channels our energy into purposeful, constructive action; a lack of discipline diffuses our energy into destructive outlets—and what we destroy the easiest and most often is ourselves.

Habits are discipline made automatic, but they're *made* automatic in the beginning and maintained via discipline. Morning routines are an example of discipline made automatic, but effective morning routines don't happen on their own. You have to set up the boundaries that create them and then stick with those boundaries via discipline.

Zooming up, picking fewer projects to finish also requires discipline. You're carrying too many projects because you've said yes to so many that you've effectively said no to making massive progress on any of them.

A major part of our resistance to discipline is that we more often associate discipline with punishment or pain than with freedom or happiness. This association is understandable since, as children, for a lot of us, discipline very often meant punishment or pain. Those experiences aren't the totality of discipline, though. The reality is that the happiest and most successful of the creatives among us are often the most disciplined. For instance, a near-universal practice among the titans and mentors that bestselling self-help author Tim Ferriss has interviewed is either a meditation practice or an exercise regimen. I've seen the same patterns among my high-achieving friends, colleagues, and clients as well. Discipline undergirds those practices and regimens, and most people report that it's *those* practices and regimens that prepare them to do their best work.

An additional upshot to discipline is that it limits the decision fatigue that plagues so many of us. A consistent morning routine eliminates scores of choices every day. Habits remove other choices. Time blocking removes more choices about when you'll do what type of work. Every decision removed from a day frees up mental and creative energy that can fuel your best work.

We're happiest when we're doing and finishing our best work, and discipline, rightly applied and cultivated, allows us to do more of our best work. As paradoxical as it sounds, discipline creates freedom and happiness precisely because it's what sets the foundation for us to do the things that matter most.

There's one skill that's so valuable that it will make you a standout in any area of life, no matter what kind of competition you face: discipline.

The discipline to show up every day, stick to the schedule, and do the work—especially when you don't feel like it—is so valuable that it's literally all you need to become better 99 percent of the time.

But what does a disciplined life actually look like?

Being disciplined means committing to what is important to you instead of merely saying something is important to you. It's about starting when you feel like stopping, not because you want to work more but rather your goal is important enough to you that you don't simply work on it when it's convenient. It's about making your priorities a reality.

Being disciplined doesn't mean you're a workaholic. It means that you're good at making time for what matters to you—especially when you don't feel like it—instead of playing the victim role and letting life happen to you.

When you start a business, there will be days when you don't feel like showing up. When you're at the gym, there will be sets that you don't feel like finishing. When it's time to write, there will be days that you don't feel like typing. But stepping up when it's annoying or painful or draining to do so, that's what makes the difference between a professional and an amateur.

Professionals have the discipline to stick to the schedule; amateurs let life get in the way.

James Clear is a habits researcher, creator of the Habits Academy, and the author of the no. 1 *New York Times* bestseller *Atomic Habits*.

HOW TO USE THE FIVE KEYS TO OVERCOME THE AIR SANDWICH

In an ideal world, each of the obstacles in the air sandwich would have one and only one key that solved it. In that same ideal world, we'd only have one obstacle at a time in front of us. In *this* world, though, we often have multiple dominant obstacles applied to different projects, and we must use multiple keys to work through them. At the same time, you'll rarely be in a situation where the lack of one key will prevent you from getting some headway when working through a project.

What follows is a rough guide for what go-to keys to start with when addressing different obstacles. It's not that you won't use others, but these keys tend to be the most effective at getting some leverage to roll the boulders out of your path.

ALIGN COMPETING PRIORITIES

Competing priorities are often the result of us not acknowledging our priorities and not seeing how our goals and plans end up at odds. Knowing that, the keys to align competing priorities are pretty straightforward:

▶ **Awareness.** Get clear about what matters to you, claim those priorities, and acknowledge that, try as you might, your reach will always exceed your grasp.

▶ **Discipline.** Keep first things first, even when it's easy to buckle.

▶ **Boundaries.** Establish structures and expectations that limit the influence of other people's priorities.

When we think of clearing our own head trash, it's normal to get a case of the "yeah, buts." It's often easier to rebut those yeahbuts by considering what you'd say to a friend grappling with the same head trash you're dealing with.

TAKE OUT YOUR HEAD TRASH

While it's true that head trash is most powerful when you can't see it for what it is, seeing it doesn't mean it just goes away. Just because something isn't true doesn't mean that it doesn't work on you. These keys will help you clear out the head trash:

▸ **Awareness.** Be aware of when self-defeating beliefs and patterns are present, and discern what's real and what's simply absorbed bullshit.

▸ **Courage.** Have the backbone to challenge those beliefs, design experiments that mitigate the patterns, and accept the reality that your choices and responses have been cocreating whatever you're experiencing.

▸ **Discipline.** Stick with challenging beliefs, experimenting, and taking responsibility to change; courage without discipline leads to fits and starts rather than deep change.

REMOVE THE *NO* FROM *NO REALISTIC PLAN*

Before we dive into the keys that will help create realistic plans, remember that plans only create clarity, not certainty. Many people make plans and feel unsatisfied because they know what they need to do but aren't sure that it will lead to success. Or they create a realistic plan and are scared they won't be able to muster their resources to do what needs to be done, so then they try to walk backward toward the project so they don't have to see what's ahead.

In the next chapter we'll see that we don't do ideas—we do projects. But sometimes you've already made a plan, in which case you'll need the following keys:

Awareness. Be aware of where you'll fall down, where you'll shine, and where you're likely to bail on the project. We'll address this in chapter 7.

Discipline. Stick with the plan when bright, shiny objects (BSOs) inevitably appear. I use "bright, shiny objects" as a shorthand for random and seemingly unlimited distractions we can spot and pounce on.

Intention. Have a clear, unmixed, and as-specific-as-useful goal or destination. As the novelist and philosopher Lewis Carroll said, "If you don't know where you are going, any road will get you there." We love to canvas all the roads in lieu of walking down one.

OVERCOME TOO FEW RESOURCES

It's very unlikely that you'll be in the position where you have all the resources you would like to have to do your best work. The more success you create, the more your best work will scale up to match your new capabilities. Learning to be resourceful regardless of how many resources you have is a lifelong skill, and these keys will show you how to use whatever you have to the fullest:

▸ **Awareness.** Focus on who and what you *do* have more than what you don't have. Ask yourself, "How can I do this project without X?" and "What do I have that I'm not using to complete this project?"

▸ **Discipline.** Efficiency requires discipline, and many of us aren't using what we have efficiently. How might you better use the resources you already have?

▸ **Courage.** Be courageous enough to commit more fully to fewer projects. We often don't focus our resources on fewer goals and projects because we're not sure that we'll be successful with those projects and thus want to hedge our bets. The result is that we invest too little into projects to make them successful and we're perennially scattered. How would you use your resources if you weren't hedging bets?

Courage. Fear. Failure. Confidence.

Our lives revolve around these words, but we have no idea what they mean.

You don't know. I don't know.

Here's a new definition for all four, one that will give you way more relief and hope and—bonus—a better future: **practice**.

The problem isn't *just* that our self-talk sucks.

The real problem is we **practice** "I'm not good enough." "Who am I to do this?" "I can't do this." We do this a thousand times a day, every day.

One day turns into three. Ten. Six weeks.

Soon we're someone who just *does that*; we think things are impossible. Our brain knows and sets its needle to No Risk.

Of course we don't send the email. Or speak at the meeting. Or pitch our idea.

How can we? All we *do* is practice telling ourselves stories *about* ourselves.

Dishonest stories that make us feel small and dead inside.

That's the muscle we're *choosing* to build every day.

What if instead of wondering if we had courage, we just practiced it instead?

Instead of worrying if we'd fail, we just exercised our mind to take the risk anyway?

What if all day, every day—one day, three days, ten days—*all* we did was take our brain to the gym? The mental gym. Work out how we'll take risks. Burn our take-action muscles, not our shame muscles. Rack up reps on confidence and positive self-talk.

Make the ask. Send the email. Get scared. Screw it up. Do it again. And again and again. Until *that* becomes your brain's new default.

What if we got our mind in shape for the race we *want* to run, not the one we're running right now?

An unconventional storyteller and brand builder, Ishita Gupta pushes levers in media, business, and publishing to connect high performers to brands and resources. As head of hoopla for Seth Godin, Ishita helped launch five bestselling books for Seth, Steven Pressfield, Derek Sivers, and more and sold the first Kindle sponsorship for Al Pittampalli's *Read This Before Our Next Meeting*. Ishita founded Fear.less magazine, profiling leading authors, thinkers, and entrepreneurs on overcoming fear. She speaks around the United States on risk-taking, leadership, mindset, performance, and confidence.

GET YOUR TEAM TO WORK WITH AND FOR YOU

An aligned team makes the difference between rowing in circles and having the wind at your back. Given that people have their own plans and can't read others' minds, it's up to you to get them working with and for you. Here are the keys that will help with that:

▸ **Awareness.** Be aware of what you *really* want, need, and dream to do and be; and be able to communicate this clearly to others. Doing so is harder than most people think it is.

▸ **Boundaries.** Establish expectations, structures, and space to support your goals. Turn *someday*, *someone*, and *sometime* into a *specific* day, person, and time.

▸ **Courage.** Be brave enough to take up space, ask for help, and stop being the martyr so people will like you.

WHICH KEYS DO YOU NEED TO PRACTICE MORE?

Your upbringing, education, experiences, choices, and preferences heavily influence which keys you cultivate and which could use some more practice. You may undercultivate or overcultivate a particular key in some areas over others. For instance, in a lot of areas, discipline is easy for me, but I've always struggled to build a running habit or avoid potatoes. Similarly, I have no problem mustering the courage for public speaking, sales, or sharing my work in public, but I'll only sing and play guitar in front of people I really trust to see me when I'm *that* vulnerable despite getting enough feedback that I'm good enough to not be embarrassed.

In my experience, though, most people know which keys they've cultivated and which they need to practice more.

Remember, the keys are just habits and practices that we get better at the more we use them; they're not innate talents we're born with (or without). Telling yourself that you can't draw boundaries, for instance, is choosing not to practice doing so.

The more you practice the keys, the easier it will be to start finishing your best work and thrive. The keys are both the obstacle and the way to your best work, depending on what you choose to practice. And, speaking of choosing to practice, it's time to practice the five keys and choose an idea that matters to you.

CHAPTER 2 TAKEAWAYS

▸ The air sandwich is the gap between your big picture and your day-to-day reality.

▸ The air in the sandwich is actually filled by five challenges that keep you from doing your best work: competing priorities, head trash, no realistic plan, too few resources, and poor team alignment.

▸ The five challenges work in concert and can show up in different ways in different projects.

▸ There are five keys to doing your best work: intention, awareness, boundaries, courage, and discipline (mnemonic: IABCD).

▸ Some keys are more effective at overcoming specific challenges than others.

▸ The five keys are practices that can be cultivated, and we're often well cultivated in some but not others.

The day came when the risk to remain tight in a bud was more painful than the risk it took to blossom.

ELIZABETH APPELL, in a promotional pamphlet for John F. Kennedy University, 1979

PICK AN IDEA THAT MATTERS TO YOU

We're paradoxical creatures. On the one hand, we all want to do our best work. On the other hand, we often avoid doing it.

This paradox only makes sense when we acknowledge that there's a lot happening in our inner landscapes that's keeping us from choosing to do our best work—and that makes choosing an idea that matters tricky. Unfortunately, with all the meetings, commutes, notifications, and things to do, we're not often privy to everything that's happening inside our hearts and minds.

What we *can* often see is that we're doing a lot of work around our best work but not getting anywhere with it. Hours, days, and weeks can go by with us researching, mulling, procrastinating, and touching our best work just enough to keep it warm but not enough to push it along.

To pick an idea that matters, the part of you that wants to thrive and do your best work will have to overcome the part of you that wants to play it safe, be comfortable, and not ruffle any feathers. It's time to embrace the thrashing you're doing.

THE MORE IT MATTERS, THE MORE YOU'LL THRASH

Thrashing is the term I use for this emotional flailing and metawork we do when we don't fully commit to our best work. What's really going on is that we're working out our own head trash—the fears, impostor syndrome, and (sometimes) unconscious perceptions of our own inadequacies. When we're thrashing, we're like the rocking chair that moves a lot but doesn't actually get anywhere.

But generating all that motion can be more exhausting than actually making progress. Even worse, at some level, we *know* we're thrashing and can't figure out why.

Here's the thing, though: we don't thrash about taking out the trash or doing the dishes. We don't have an existential crisis of varying degrees of intensity when it's time to cook dinner or go to the library. (Though if you're anything like me, having to decide which books won't be going home with you can invoke a mini crisis.)

If you're familiar with Steven Pressfield's notion of resistance, you might think that thrashing and resistance are the same thing. They're not. Resistance is the inner voice or actor that's often the mouthpiece for all the head trash we carry with us. Thrashing is what we do in response to resistance.

That may seem like a minor difference, but what I find useful in the distinction is that we can notice when we're thrashing and decide that we're going to *do* something different, even as the resistance yells at us ever more loudly and forcefully. Additionally, knowing about thrashing allows us to tell others what thrashing looks like for us so they can call us on it, rather than leave it for them to guess what's going on inside our head and heart.

We only thrash about the things that matter to us: getting married for the first (or third) time; leaving a comfortable job to start our own business; writing a book; starting a nonprofit; doing an open-mic event; sharing our art with a new audience; kicking off a disruptive strategic project. Each of these can get us thrashing, and many people never actually get beyond thrashing.

The more an idea matters to you, the more you'll thrash, precisely because its success or failure is deeply important to you.

While most of us don't care about how perfectly aligned our trash cans are when we put them out on the curb, we *do* care about how perfectly presented our best work is. Our best work is a representation of our internal character, competency, and excellence in a way that the curbside trash cans aren't. (At least, that's the story we tell ourselves.)

Every project that matters to us will entail some thrashing, but where we'll thrash is often quite particular to us.

Some of us thrash:

▷ **Before we start working on an idea.** "Who am I to do this project?" "Does this project even matter?" "Is this original enough?" "Can I actually do this?"

▷ **In the middle of the project.** "How the hell do I get this project back on track?" "Why is this project so hard for me?" "Is anyone even going to care if I finish this?" "Is this really the best thing I can be doing right now?"

▷ **At the end of the project.** "Is this good enough?" "What will people think of me?" "What about the haters, trolls, and naysayers?" "What if I miss something important?"

▷ **Throughout every stage of a project.** We're masters of the flailathon.

A natural response to thrashing is to pick easier ideas to work on. Sheer exhaustion, frustration, and the desire to actually get something done make switching projects seem like a good idea. Ain't nobody got time to wear themselves out for half of the day and not have anything to show for it.

You're most likely to start reaching for an easier project when your project goes into a void. When your project is in a void, it can seem like it can keep going nowhere forever and there's not a clear way to get the project out of the void. Best-work projects are particularly prone to have one or more voids, which is yet another reason they too easily get pushed to the side for an easier project.

Beware the siren call of the "easier" idea, though. If you switch to an easier project that matters, you'll end up thrashing anyway, and it will probably be in about the same spot as the current project you're thrashing with. It's not like switching to an easier project automagically means you've addressed what caused you to thrash with your previous one. And if it's an easier project, you *might* finish it, but you won't feel nearly as satisfied as if you had finished the one you bailed on. And you'll still be haunted by whatever undone project you switched from.

Thrashing is thus not a sign that you can't finish the project or that you're doing the wrong project. It's a sign that you're doing something that matters to you and that you'll need to show up powerfully to get it done. It's also not something you'll ever get away from—as you become more powerful and accomplished, the ideas you'll grapple with will scale with you, in scope, breadth, or difficulty.

AVOIDING YOUR BEST WORK
LEADS TO CREATIVE CONSTIPATION

Your best work is always going to be challenging because it's the work that matters to you. And because it matters to you, you're going to be thrashing along the way. Best work is starting to look suspiciously like hard work, and our natural reaction is to avoid doing hard work and to instead find something easier to do.

When it comes to your best work, *not* doing it comes with two major costs: (1) you won't be able to thrive, and (2) you'll be stricken with creative constipation. Since I've already discussed the link between thriving and your best work, let's talk about *creative constipation*, or the pain of not doing your best work.

Creative constipation is exactly what it sounds like. We take in ideas and inspiration that get converted into aspirations, goals, and projects, and at a certain point, if we're not pushing them out in the form of finished projects, they start to back up on us.

And like physical constipation, at a certain point, we get toxic. We don't want to take in any more ideas. We don't want to do any more projects. We don't want to set any more goals or plans. We're full and fed up.

That inner toxicity becomes the broth that flavors all our stories about ourselves and the world; our head trash gets more pronounced and intense, and what we see in the world goes from bright to dark. Creative constipation leads to behaviors in which we lash out at the world—and sometimes even more intensely at ourselves. We become resentful of others—even people we love—who are doing their best work. Our ability to feel positive emotional peaks is diminished at the same time that our ability to feel negative emotional troughs is amplified. You've no doubt encountered the tortured, depressed soul who's creatively constipated—and you may have been there yourself.

There's a reason that nearly every spiritual tradition links creativity and destruction: the same energy that fuels creation also fuels destruction. The Jewish, Christian, and Muslim God creates and destroys; "beating swords into plowshares" works equally in reverse. The Hindu god Shiva is seen as a destroyer who makes way for creativity. Creativity and destruction are seen as a continual loop in the Taoist concept of yin and yang.

Spiritual insights such as these also show up in our everyday lives. Think about how often you've engaged in retail therapy—and thus destroyed your time and resources—because you're unsatisfied about something in your life. Think about how often you've indulged in emotional eating because you're not creating the change you want to see in your life. Think about how many people blow up their lives in a midlife crisis because the career and life they've made haven't satisfied their deep needs.

Now think about the people you know or have read about who *are* doing their best work. Notice how they're healthier, happier, (usually) more financially comfortable, and in good relationships with others? Doing their best work creates meaning for them at the same time that it cocreates who they want to be in the world. And these folks know that doing their work *in the world* is the wheel of change, meaning, and growth, more so than merely being stuck in their heads.

So at both deep and practical levels, we can choose to channel our energy to do our best work and thrive, or we can choose to leave it unharnessed to gradually destroy ourselves, our relationships, our resources, and the world around us. Better to do the hard work of creation than the hard work of repairing the destruction we've wrought.

WE ARE MADE TO SLAY DRAGONS

Your best work is hard work during which you'll thrash, and if you don't do the work, you'll be feeling a different kind of pain. "There be dragons" on the journey to thriving and doing your best work. You can avoid some of the dragons—especially the ones you create for yourself—but you shouldn't expect to avoid all of them.

It's far better to be skeptical about doing the easy work or always picking the low-hanging fruit. Too many of us wake up after doing years of work that doesn't stretch us or make us really show up to do it, and we realize that we've been phoning it in. Easy work can be like fast food: it's quick, easy, and cheap, but it's not fulfilling and too much of it can lead to dis-ease.

But here's the deal: we are made to slay dragons. We have survived for hundreds of thousands of years using our creativity, grit, imagination, and cooperative spirit. We've harnessed fire and metal and the very energy of the universe to alter reality. We've survived countless plagues, wars, and famines. Physically, we're the weakest and least capable of every predator and yet we're the apex predator on this planet.

We're simply the latest in the line of generations of dragon slayers. We're resilient, adaptable, ingenious, and triumphant folk.

So what if there are a few dragons on this journey? They have always been there and likely always will be there. Lesser people than us have tussled with them and won, and we can too.

Dragons aren't a signal that we're on the wrong road but rather that we're on the *right* road. So the next time you're dismayed or hesitant because of a dragon guarding the way forward, embrace that it's there precisely because it's the way forward and charge headlong at it. You were made to beat dragons.

THE GIFT OF FAILURE

You may be made to slay dragons, but it doesn't mean you'll always be able to do so. Failure is inevitable, and if you're not failing and making the occasional bad decision, you're not doing your best work. *Really* showing up and dancing with the uncertainty that comes with doing your best work means you're going to underestimate, underprioritize, and underprepare for a challenge that then gets the best of you.

But failure isn't a mark of character but rather a sign that something was out of alignment. Maybe you . . .

▷ Charged ahead by yourself rather than asking for help.

▷ Said yes too quickly when you were already overcommitted.

▷ Had a streak of easy wins that unlocked a new level of challenge that you weren't ready for.

▷ Chose an idea that didn't match your actual priorities, and the projects that relate to your priorities won out.

▷ Put the wrong people on your team for the wrong reasons.

▷ Needed to spend more time honing your skills or collecting your resources.

▷ Had a beautiful plan that reality shattered in wonderful or terrible ways you couldn't anticipate.

Your past failures are in the past. They aren't predictive of what you'll be able to do in the future. Your best bet is to follow this Cherokee proverb: don't let yesterday eat up too much of today.

But that's not to say the sting of failure isn't real. A corollary of "the more it matters, the more you'll thrash" is that the more it matters to you, the more it will sting when you fail. This truth is another reason we choose to avoid our best work.

CHELSEA DINSMORE   WHAT TO DO WHEN LIFE CHANGES YOUR PLANS

There are many things in life out of our control, and when life changes our plans it's hard not to feel helpless. I learned this the hard way when my husband, Scott, was killed in an accident while we were hiking Mount Kilimanjaro. Not only was I having to process this sudden and tragic loss but I was also doing it in front of the global community we had built. What happened was out of my control, but my *response* to it was not.

This is why I encourage people to have a practice that allows them to intentionally *respond* rather than simply *react* to any given situation. We must first accept that what happens around us isn't what dictates our feelings; it's our *thoughts* that create them. We go in and out of emotions based on our thoughts, which often come as a result of what we focus on. Our circumstances may be facts, but our emotions are fleeting—focusing on what we can't do creates hopelessness; focusing on what we can do creates motivation.

When we begin to notice the thoughts that create painful and pleasurable emotions, we reveal patterns, understand triggers, and gain insight into where we can better direct our focus in any given moment. The better we can learn to manage our minds, rather than react to them, the better we can handle any situation, regardless of the level of difficulty.

This is a power no circumstance can take away from you!

Chelsea Dinsmore is the owner of Live Your Legend, a business that helps people discover how to live their lives with a deeper sense of purpose, meaning, and mindfulness.

The gift of failure is that it reveals what matters to you, shows you when you're out of alignment, and reveals a growth edge.

Each day is a new day to try again with the lessons of yesterday as a guide, not a straitjacket.

Failure is thus like that friend who tells you what you need to hear rather than what you want to hear. But it's not the only friend keeping you on your game.

DISPLACEMENT IS YOUR FRIEND (AFTER IT'S YOUR ENEMY)

One of the biggest dragons seems to be time. There's never enough, and we don't get it back.

The more years I spend on this planet, the more I see that we *need* the constraint of finite time for the meaning making that matters the most to us. That constraint creates *displacement*, and taking displacement seriously allows us to make better choices. Displacement is simply the reality that every action we choose to do displaces countless others we could have done in the same space and time.

That's all very general and spiritual, I know. To make it more concrete, let's consider *Whole Earth Catalog* creator Stewart Brand's idea that significant, impactful ideas will require at least five years of focused action to complete.[1] Subtract your current age from eighty-five and divide by five—that's how many significant projects you have left to do.

---

1. *Wired* magazine founder Kevin Kelly attributed this to Stewart Brand in Tim Ferriss's *Tools of Titans: The Tactics, Routines, and Habits of Billionaires, Icons, and World-Class Performers* (New York: Houghton Mifflin Harcourt, 2016).

By the time this book is published, I'll be cresting forty, so that means I have nine significant projects left. That's only so many nonprofit boards I can serve on, pillars of my body of work that I can build, ways I can serve my community and nation, and places I might move to and truly experience. Yes, knowing I only have nine buckets to pour my life energy into feels like the universe is sitting on my chest. But it also makes me extra discerning about what significant projects I choose to do and how my days go toward those projects.

No matter how we choose to spend our hours, we each get twenty-four of them each day. That finite limit is a hellish constraint for many of us.

But that finite limit can be a gift of heaven just the same. Consider how much more we waste when we have more to waste. How many times have you looked back over a day or week that had *too much* unplanned time and been frustrated that you squandered that time precisely because it was too open? Or how many times have you clicked over to Facebook because you were bored—that is, you had open time where you weren't engaged?

Another major gift of displacement is that it can help you assess the cost of being spread across too many projects and responsibilities. For example, I'd like to write more than one book every five years, but to do so, I'll have to do like other prolific authors and cut more things out of my life to do so. If I decide to cut or not take on something that consumes ten hours per week, I could then apply those ten hours to a book. In that scenario, I'd be able to write one book a year pretty easily. There's even a helpful constraint there as well, in that there's only so much creative energy available per day and it's *far* less than many people think.

We could quibble about whether Brand's correct about impactful ideas taking five years to complete or what counts as a significant project, but doing so wouldn't change the fact that we have a finite amount of time and whatever we do in that time displaces other things we might do.

As you get better at using the five keys and focusing on your best work, displacement will become an even better friend. When stuff that really doesn't matter and isn't worth your time, energy, and attention shows up, you'll *feel* it right away, and you'll also feel the potential cost of letting your current project go. We're wired to feel the pain of loss more than the pleasure of possible gains. *Losing* the grip and momentum you're currently building will make it easier to wick away the drops of nonmeaningful stuff as if it were water on a rain jacket. Your fear of missing out (FOMO) will shift from missing out on what other people are doing to missing out on what *you* could be doing with time well used.

But in the beginning you'll fight and thrash against displacement. That's just the infinite part of yourself straining against its bindings. Part of the struggle of the human condition is being an unlimited sentience trapped in a limited body; part of the beauty of the human condition is being an unlimited sentience that gets to use its power through space and time.

I'm highlighting this tension with displacement because we're heading toward a choice that will catalyze that tension. At the end of this chapter I'll ask you to pick one idea to start working on and to use it as the lens to understand the ideas ahead. You'll likely struggle with choosing, and a major part of that struggle may be resistance to the premise that you have to or should choose.

When that time and struggle come, remember these three things:

▸ Everything you do displaces something else you could have done.

▸ The work that *really* matters will require a concerted amount of time to finish.

▸ The more you channel your energy toward one project, the faster you'll finish it and therefore can move on to the next project.

Not choosing is a choice that costs you far more in the long run than choosing and finishing one significant project at a time. We can't run away from displacement, but we *can* use it to start finishing our best work.

TO TRADE UP, YOU HAVE TO LET GO

While we're on displacement, it's useful to think about all the ideas and projects you're carrying and what they're displacing. You're currently carrying a mixed bag of projects and responsibilities, the majority of which aren't related to your best work or the activities and ideas that are most going to move you toward thriving. The minority of stuff that's close-ish to your best work is likely stagnant, existing in the same progress status as that closet you stuff full of things you don't want to process right now but can't outright get rid of.

I'm not judging. As I've been saying all along, it's far too easy for stuff that doesn't matter to end up on your to-do list while the stuff that *does* matter languishes as you wait for days where you won't have the rest of the stuff to do. Those days are coming, we all swear, despite the lifelong evidence that they won't.

While we *will* begin to eliminate some of the work that doesn't matter, we'll need to start with that closet of ideas and projects we really want to do. This may seem like a counterintuitive place to start. Wouldn't starting with the bigger list of stuff that doesn't matter as much give the biggest bang for the buck? After all, if it's 80 percent of where our time is going, and we remove 25 percent of it, then we can apply that time, energy, and attention to the stuff in the closet, right?

Probably not, for two reasons. First, the stuff that's currently on our list is there for a reason, and if it were so easy to let go of, we would have done it already. We either had it imposed upon us or we accepted it at some point in the past. In either case, it has *some* energy and story attached to it, and it will take some active effort to dissipate the energy and rewrite the story.

The second reason why it's unlikely that we'll automagically start doing our best work is because our existing pattern is to fill the space with stuff that doesn't matter as much. If you're a people-pleaser, you're more likely to fill that space with stuff that "pays off" the people-pleasing you haven't been doing because you've been too busy. If you're a perfectionist, you're more likely to go about shoring up something you feel you half-did in the past, regardless of whether it's still alive or not.

If we don't consciously make the effort to change things, our default habits and patterns will keep filling the holes we make. We have to *start* by filling those holes with work that does matter. This is how displacement can be a gift. We can put something that's harder to displace in those cracks and holes, and, with practice, we can replace the go-to chicken wire and duct tape of ephemera with the more solid brick and mortar of our best work.

But to get some headway with your best work, you have to fight the natural inclination to work on *all the things* you've hidden away in that closet. That road ends with your being unsatisfied by your lack of progress and focus, with a strong possibility that you'll just shove even more undone stuff back in the closet. You've probably walked this road before and don't want to walk it again.

Instead, you must decide from the get-go that you're just going to let some of those ideas go.

The best way to finish something is often to just drop it, midstream and undone, even while feeling the sting of remorse, regret, and sadness of not seeing it through.

And let's not pretend as if the choice of letting some of those projects and ideas go is primarily a mental activity. It's an emotional activity—your soul, emotions, and creative energy are tied up in those ideas. Sometimes there's money and social skin in the game as well, and none of us want to walk away from money we've sunk into something or feel the shame of not seeing our commitments through. Better to hold on to them, as you might get around to them someday.

This reminds me of my dad, a brilliant and industrious jack-of-all-trades. Dad would often salvage things from the construction sites and jobs he worked on because he was "fixin' to" use them on some unspecified project he was going to work on. He'd kept almost every vehicle he ever owned because he was "fixin' to" fix them up and use them. He's going on eighty and currently has dementia, and my siblings and I are left with over an acre of stuff collected over the last sixty years that Dad never could let go of because he just knew someday all that "fixin' to" would turn into something he actually did. Even now, on bad days, he thinks about all that stuff and how he's going to get to those projects. How much of his soul is tied up in things he'll never get to?

My father is a product of his time, when physical stuff was what was collected in order to build real stuff in the world. In the near eighty years since he was born, our society has shifted from atoms to bits—to use entrepreneur, TED Conference curator, and author Chris Anderson's phraseology.[2] More of us work in intangibles, including services, than in tangibles anymore. We don't have an acre of unprocessed stuff, but we have the same analogous amount of space in our souls occupied with things we're "fixin' to" get to.

In the next section, I'll be asking you to pick one idea or project to work on or use as an anchor to apply the insights from this book. But in this section I'm asking you to pick some ideas that you *won't* be working on anymore so you can free up that energy to fuel what you do work on. It's a hard ask now, but it will make the next exercise easier because you'll be working with a shorter list.

So let's start to unpack that closet of ideas and projects. Here's how I suggest doing this:

2. See Chris Anderson, *Free: The Past and Future of a Radical Price* (New York: Hyperion, 2009).

- **Give yourself two uninterrupted hours for this exercise.**

- **Do it somewhere other than where you work most of the time.** Coffee shops and libraries are particularly good settings.

- **Use a pencil and paper.** Use a pencil so you can erase when you need to—and you'll need to. Use paper so you don't collapse into fiddling with technology and checking stuff that doesn't need to be checked right now.

Mindmapping can be more useful than a linear list, but this is *not* the time to learn how to mindmap if you're not familiar with the process.

- **List all of the ideas and projects you want to do.** Think beyond "professional" ideas and projects—yard and house projects, community initiatives, events with your community, traveling to Nepal, sorting your finances, or getting a puppy all count. It can be items on your bucket list, but they don't have to be bucket-list level.

Once you have this list, start asking yourself the following questions and put an asterisk behind items that meet the criteria of the questions:

1 **Which of the items wouldn't actually hurt at all if you cut them?** Be on the lookout for projects and ideas that some previous version of yourself put there that aren't relevant for where you are right now. For instance, this could be a degree or certificate to get a job you no longer want or that you already have. It could be a creative project that past-you desperately needed to prove yourself that current-you no longer needs because you're no longer seeking approval.

2 **Which of the items would you feel relieved to no longer be carrying?** Pay more attention to how it will feel once it's no longer on your

plate than to what you would need to do to let go of it.

3 **Which of the items are "shoulds" or items that relate to OPP (other people's priorities), but you don't see how they'll directly lead to your thriving?**

4 **Which of the items are good ideas but don't relate to something that frustrates, annoys, angers, inspires, nourishes, or calls to you?** You can't build the flame to temper your project from a good idea that doesn't have an emotional spark to start with.

SUSAN PIVER   SHOULD YOU BREAK UP WITH YOUR IDEA?

Conventional wisdom says that success is dependent on your intelligence, skill, drive, connections, and resilience. Should you encounter obstacles, just work harder. When things seem hopeless, hustle more. Eventually your idea is bound to work.

But this is simply not true. There's something missing from this view.

Obstacles aren't merely stumbling blocks to be gotten around; they're a source of wisdom. Sometimes the wisdom shows you a better way, but sometimes—and this can be very hard to accept—the wisdom is telling you to stop. Give up. Move on.

How do you know when you should push harder or let go? To discover the answer, it's useful to take yourself out of the center of the equation. We all think our work is about us and our talents and aspirations. It turns out that this is only partially true, because

in order for your project or idea to work, it has to, at some point, *spark*. A relationship with the world—whether that world is the consumer marketplace, a business sector, or a single client—has to arise.

Ideas are like blind dates. Either may appear perfect on paper—smart, interesting, and attractive—but if there's no chemistry, it won't work. You can go out on a million more dates, but that will never change. It's a matter of history, timing, and the mysteries of destiny. What looks good on the surface is only the beginning.

When the world falls in love with your work, you'll know it. In the meantime, stay strong and confident in yourself, but develop the capacity to read the signs clearly, respond fearlessly, and remain open to what comes next. It may be better than you ever dreamed.

Susan Piver is a Buddhist teacher and the *New York Times* bestselling author of nine books. She is founder of the Open Heart Project, the largest virtual mindfulness community in the world.

If you really engage with the questions, you'll be able to eliminate a lot of items from your list. How many depends on how long you've crammed stuff in that closet without purging it. If you're a frequent purger, you may have a short list. If it's been a while, you may have a long list.

Now the important part:

eliminate those items rather than defer and put them back in the closet later.

Whenever that later comes, they'd be asterisked all over again. You've done the hard work of making the evaluation once—don't do it again.

Some people find it helpful to do a send-off process for each item. Think about the item, how you came to it, how it's helped you, and how sending it off will open up more energy for something that's relevant now. A simpler process would be to say something such as "I release you" or "we're complete." Burning the list has been particularly cathartic for me and others I've led through a similar process. How you do it is less important than making the clean, intentional break.

Now that you've let go of stuff that matters less, you can trade up to what matters more. To prep for that, rewrite the list you started with so that it only includes ideas and projects that made the cut. For the projects you've let go, there's no need to see them anymore.

FIVE QUESTIONS TO HELP YOU SORT THROUGH WHAT MATTERS MOST

If you did the exercise above, you may have been surprised to see that what you originally thought was important to you really wasn't, and what you pushed aside as unimportant really was. If you've experienced a roller coaster of emotions, great—that means you've been open and honest with yourself. You're right where you should be.

Much as we learn to live by living, we learn to do our best work by doing our best work. And the best way to do our best work is to pick a specific idea to work on, which means it's time to choose that specific idea. Your task is a lot easier if you followed the exercise above and have let go of ideas and projects that aren't as important. A bunch of little, less important ideas can add up to overwhelm in the same way that a bunch of little, less important requests can.

Before we get to the questions that will help you pick the one idea to work on, know that "not now" isn't the same thing as "no." By picking one idea, you'll be saying "not now" to others—this is displacement in effect—and it can often feel like "not now" means the same thing as "no." Intentionally not working on an idea typically feels more uncomfortable than unintentionally not working on it, but deciding not to work on an idea frees up that energy and focus to intentionally finish and work on another. Better to use the five keys (especially courage and discipline) to intentionally finish one idea than to not use them and unintentionally not finish a bunch.

You may also avoid choosing because you're afraid you'll pick the wrong thing. Remember, if you finish the idea sooner, you can move on to something else sooner without the baggage and debt of the current idea and will thus finish the next idea faster.

Take the short list from the section above and use the following five questions to pick the project that matters most.

1 Imagine that you're celebrating with a friend or loved one the most important thing you've done over the last year. If you could only pick one of the items on the list, which would it be?

2 Which of the items on the list causes the most gut-level anguish when you consider cutting it from the list completely? If you're not sure of what I mean by gut-level anguish, imagine your most cherished object being destroyed in a fire. Which item, if removed, causes *that* feeling the most?

3 Which of the items on the list are you most likely to wake up for two hours earlier, stay up for two hours later, or steal time elsewhere to create two hours to do?

4 Which of the items on the list, if finished, will matter the most in five years, in terms of having done it or how it sets up your future self for thriving?

5 Which of the items on the list is worth claiming one of your remaining "significant project" slots? Recall from the section on displacement that you have a number of significant project slots equal to (85 minus your age) divided by 5 (rounded down).

Ideally one idea will emerge as the clear winner, but in the real world, one or three might be relatively tied depending on which of the questions gets the most weight. In the case of this kind of tie, go with the idea that wins on question 3, not because question 3 is the most important one, all things considered, but because it's better to get momentum on one idea that you'll create time for than others that you won't.

Once you've made the choice, do the following three steps:

1 Circle the idea you've chosen to work on.

2 Put a date on the top of the piece of paper you've been working from so you know when you made this choice.

3 Take a picture of the piece of paper so you have a digital record of it and put the physical piece of paper someplace where you'll see it a few times a week. This could be on a corkboard or whiteboard, your refrigerator, or framed on your desk.

The three steps above will free up a significant amount of energy in the long run because (a) you won't have to make the choice again; (b) if you lose your list, you have a backup; and (c) you'll be reminded of the ideas you *didn't* choose at the same time that they'll get some background incubation while you're finishing the one you did. The few minutes it will take to do the three steps above will give you weeks and months in the future.

It's time to start finishing your idea. If "finishing an idea" sounds funny, you're ahead of the game, for we don't do ideas, we do *projects*. Converting your idea into a doable project that you'll finish is what we're getting into next.

CHAPTER 3 TAKEAWAYS

▸ The more something matters to you, the more you'll thrash, precisely because its success or failure is deeply important to you.

▸ Not doing your best work leads to creative constipation—at a certain point, you're too toxic to take new ideas in because you're not getting them out.

▸ We are but the latest in the line of gritty problem-solvers—we were made to slay dragons.

▸ The gift of failure is that it reveals what matters to you, shows you when you're out of alignment, and reveals a growth edge.

▸ Displacement—the fact that doing something now excludes doing anything else—can help you focus on what matters, but only after you accept the limitations of time and energy.

▸ You have to let go of projects and ideas that aren't allowing you to thrive so you can trade up to the projects that do.

▸ "Not now" isn't the same thing as "no."

PART 2

PLANNING YOUR PROJECT

The ability to convert ideas to things
is the secret to outward success.
HENRY WARD BEECHER,
Proverbs from Plymouth Pulpit

CONVERT YOUR IDEA INTO A PROJECT

Now that you've chosen an idea that matters, you're *much* closer to doing your best work. It may have been hard work to pick that idea, but by doing so, you've given yourself something compelling enough that you'll stick to it until the end.

It's time for you to take your idea and convert it to a project that you can make space for and start talking about with people who are going to help you see it through. Since we do projects, not ideas, let's start by looking at where the project is taking you.

CONVERT YOUR IDEA INTO A SMART GOAL

Being stuck with an idea that's not yet a goal keeps you swimming in the ocean of possibility, which is fun for a little while but exhausting over the long term. Converting that idea into a goal gives you a safe shore to swim to.

But it turns out that some formulations of goals get us to done better than others.

Consider the following two formulations of the same goal:

▸ Book
▸ Complete a book on the history of cappuccino by the end of 2019

Which of the two are more likely to get done? Our survey says the second.

That may seem to be a straw-man comparison, but my work with thousands of creative folks shows that many goals look closer to the first than the second. The more distant the goal seems to be, the more it looks like the first. Consider, for example, the "saving for retirement" goal you likely have. Does it provide the details you need to prioritize, implement, and track your progress toward it? How much is enough? And so on.

A SMART goal[1] formulation that works particularly well for creative people is a variation of a framework you may have seen at time-management seminars. While the standard framework works well in some contexts—especially those in which you're on the receiving end of a goal—it doesn't work quite as well for creative projects and creative folks.

The variation of the SMART framework I recommend is:

▸ Simple   ▸ Actionable   ▸ Trackable
▸ Meaningful   ▸ Realistic

---

1. George T. Doran first formulated the SMART goal framework in "There's a S.M.A.R.T. Way to Write Management's Goals and Objectives," *Management Review* 70, no. 11 (November 1981): 35–36.

Let's handle each in turn:

IS YOUR GOAL SIMPLE?

A goal is simple when you can look at it without wondering. You shouldn't have to look up something else to understand its meaning.

Simple doesn't necessarily mean that it's easy, but simply stated goals help you know exactly what you need to do to move forward with the idea. If you look at a goal and have to think about what you need to do to count that goal as done, your goal isn't simple.

When we set a complicated goal for the future, it may be difficult to hold on to its meaning over time. A complicated goal made when we're in the zone may be harder to understand when we're not—the last thing we want to do first thing in the morning is struggle to figure out what we're supposed to be doing, and knowing that we're retreading ground we've already trod makes it more frustrating. Simple goals help set us up for success.

As we'll see in a moment, simple and actionable are often related: actionable goals tend to be simple. That said, it's entirely possible and normal to have a goal that's simple but not actionable, or a goal that's actionable but not simple.

IS YOUR GOAL MEANINGFUL?

A goal is meaningful when you can look at it and quickly understand the importance of completing that goal.

If in the previous chapter you chose an idea that matters, you've done this already. We learned there that we're more likely to be successful with ideas that matter than with ideas that don't connect with our heads and hearts.

What often trips people up, though, is that they equate meaning and desire, but that's an unnecessary relationship: you might not *want* to do something that's meaningful, yet it still might be meaningful to do. For instance, you may not want to do your taxes, do the back-to-school shopping for the kids, or help transition your aging parent to assisted living, but these projects have meaning in the broader context of your life.

While doing enjoyable work creates pleasure, doing meaningful work creates fulfillment—and there's no reason why meaningful work can't also be enjoyable work.

IS YOUR GOAL ACTIONABLE?

A goal is actionable when it's immediately clear what action needs to be taken to accomplish the goal.

If there's nothing you can do to bring about your goal, it's not a goal—it's a wish. A wish is granted by someone or something other than you and is thus out of your control. You can't plan for it or work toward it by clearing space on your calendar. I'm all for wish lists; combining wish lists and action lists, not so much.

Making a goal actionable is perhaps the simplest criterion to meet because it's just a matter of thinking of the actions that will bring about that goal. The simplest way to make a goal actionable is to begin the phrase with a verb. Instead of "Chapter 1," phrase the goal as "Write chapter 1."

IS YOUR GOAL REALISTIC?

A goal is realistic when the endpoint is achievable with the resources you have available.

We creative folks have a lot of friction with this one, as we have that peculiar ability to change the world in important ways. To be creative is often to see parts of reality as tentative.

However, just because we can change the way things are doesn't mean we can do it *all at once* or without regard to the basic constraints of reality. Try as you might, you can't change the fact that it takes time to do things well or that you need sleep. You also can't change social reality overnight—or, if you do, it will probably be accidental.

Rather than put your head in the sand and try to deny the way things are, asking whether your goal is realistic helps you figure out ways to make it more likely that you'll succeed. Identifying drag points—those places and elements where your goal is likely to go sideways—allows you to plan ways to overcome them. Better to beat the dragon you already know is there than pretend as if it's not there and then be surprised by it.

Realistic goals and trackable goals are often heavily interrelated, especially if you track your goals based on time. An unrealistic goal can often be made realistic and doable by changing your expectation of how long you think it would and should take.

IS YOUR GOAL TRACKABLE?

A goal is trackable, quantitatively or qualitatively, when it's clear what progress means.

Most SMART-goal advocates use the *T* for "time-specific," but I prefer to leave it more open. Some goals don't fit into a temporal framework as easily as others, but it doesn't mean that we can't actively do things to bring about those goals.

Consider the broad goal of being a better friend. Setting a goal to become a better friend by June 1 is neither meaningful nor simple. However, it can be a recurring broad goal with which you check in every once in a while by asking yourself what you're doing to be a better friend to specific people. Understanding a goal in this way makes plenty of room for other kinds of uniquely human activities such as contemplation, intuition, mindfulness, and unstructured learning in ways that setting rigid time frames can unhelpfully constrain.

That said,

most goals are best formulated with time specificity; assigning a timeline to a goal can help us identify the simple actions we can take to bring about that goal at the same time that it makes the goal feel more real.

Additionally, if there's a specific quantitative measure that relates to your goal, having the courage and intention to use that measure can go a long way to creating a plan that actually succeeds. For instance, many people want to change the world for the better, but they haven't specified the number of things they want to change. "Keeping kids from going hungry" is a noble goal; "feeding one hundred thousand kids who would otherwise go hungry" is noble, simple, trackable, and compelling. (For those who just said "But what about all the other kids?" if you can't feed one hundred thousand, you can't feed all the others, so best get to work on that first one hundred thousand and upgrade as you go along.)

HOW TO MAKE YOUR GOAL SMART, STEP BY STEP

While making SMART goals comes naturally to some people, many creative people unhappily struggle with it. It's really a matter of practice; and once you practice it, you won't be able to abide a non-SMART goal. I've been doing this so long that seeing non-SMART goals creates the same effect as thinking about round squares; it actually stops my train of thought unless I correct them or stop looking at them.

From a practical point of view, the simplest way to convert your idea into a SMART goal is to add a piece at a time, with the following steps being the easiest order:

1 **Verb it!** State the goal with a verb that best captures what finishing the goal looks like. Some examples: "Move Alex to Atlanta." "Publish a book." "Rework staffing strategy." If you're stuck, use the word *finish* at this point; when you break the project down, you'll use more specific completion words.

2 **Time it!** Think about what seems to be a reasonable amount of time to complete the goal, then double that time. Why double it? To account for the fact that we chronically underestimate how long it will take to get something done. Doubling the time will help you set a realistic goal.

3 **Check it against reality.** I know you think you'll be able to do it faster than how long you just said if you doubled it, but remember, you'll be doing this project *along with other projects*, and almost all of us creative folk underestimate how long something will take and overestimate how much we'll prioritize any given goal.

4 **Reread the goal to see if it's still simple.** It will probably have some formulaic phrasing such as "Completion (Verb) (Idea) by (Date)"—for example, "Move Alex to Atlanta by June 1"—and that's a very, very good thing. Use your creativity and mental horsepower to figure out how to do the work, not to figure out what the work is.

Because we already started with an idea that matters, we already know it's meaningful.

There are three powerful upshots for choosing to consistently use the SMART framework for your goals:

▸ You'll have a default that will accelerate your ability to convert ideas into goals and push them to the finish line.

▸ You'll be able to review a list of goals with a similar format and see how they relate. If too many goals need to be completed in the same time frame, you'll be able to see that you'll need to do some deconflicting and sequencing in advance. You want to avoid the pressure-cooker pattern where everything is due all at once followed by a period of recovering from being exhausted, only to have everything due all at once all over again. Crockpot creativity leads to better work and a better life than pressure-cooker creativity.

▸ You'll be better able to communicate with other people about your goals since they'll be easy to decode and discuss.

A not-so-powerful upshot is that you, too, will experience mental misfiring when you see a non-SMART goal. You're welcome.

Take a look at the idea you chose in the last chapter. How can you rewrite that goal to make it SMART?

Fair warning: When you convert that idea into a SMART goal, you may experience some tension and anxiety. You may be questioning if your goal is realistic or you're eager to take action on it but you're stumbling with some of the elements of the air sandwich. Excitement, tension, frustration, and other hard-to-pin-down emotions are all normal and sure signs that you're grappling with something that matters to you.

THE THREE LEVELS OF SUCCESS

A chief challenge in converting an idea into a SMART goal is figuring out what success looks like. We tend to bifurcate our outcomes into success or failure, but this is an oversimplistic view. There are *levels* of success, and which level of success you choose should weigh heavily into the plan you make to achieve that goal.

Before we go into the levels of success, one of the best things you can do when you start planning is to assume you'll succeed rather than assume you'll fail. While we all *want* to be successful, many of us start planning as if we're going to fail. We spend a lot of energy and time imagining what failure looks like, so much so that we build a plan that focuses on preventing failure rather than setting up success. The end result is that we choose smaller goals and less ambitious projects that ultimately don't fulfill us because they never require us to channel the courage and discipline to do what we're most capable of. Consider the best-work project in front of you and how planning to prevent failure feels different than planning to succeed.

Since we're focusing on success, I won't focus much on the levels of failure. Let's consider three different levels of success:

Small Success. Since tests are the easiest analogy, consider a small success as getting the minimum score needed to pass. The thing about small successes is that we're never really proud of accruing them, but a string of small successes done with coherence and intention can lead to much greater success down the line. So even though we may not be proud of them, they're still successes and worth celebrating.

Moderate Success. A moderate success exceeds the minimum requirements for success. While you may not be shouting from the rooftops about a moderate success, you're likely to be proud of the outcome. Moderate success is the highest level of success you can achieve with just your own effort, resources, and advantages.

Epic Success. If you're not a Millennial or younger, you can substitute *extreme* for *epic*. An epic success greatly exceeds the minimum requirements for success and is a "tell your momma" moment. It's your version of getting on *The Oprah Winfrey Show* or winning the Super Bowl. Epic success requires you to build a team to help you get there.

Considering the levels of success while goal setting helps you align your expectations and resources. Small successes don't require nearly as much effort and focus as epic successes, but many of us want epic success with small-success-level effort and focus. Additionally, having epic success across all dimensions of our lives requires intention, awareness, boundaries, courage, and discipline at mastery levels not yet reached by most of us.

Applying the levels of success also wards off the low-level insanity, anxiety, and overwhelm that so many of us grapple with every day because we're expecting higher levels of success across all dimensions of our lives without doing the work to get to those levels of success. If you aim for a small success from the beginning, you can actually be satisfied when you achieve it. If you aim for epic success from the beginning, when things get hard—and at this level, they will get hard—you can remind yourself that it's not hard because something's wrong with you but more simply because you chose to play at a level that really makes you show up.

Let's make this less abstract so it has more grip. Consider the fuzzy goal of running a marathon. A small success might be finishing the marathon, which could include walking parts of it and finishing before the event ends. A moderate success might be running the whole way. An epic success might be winning your category. It's pretty obvious in this example that there's a big difference in what it's going to take to succeed at these different levels; depending on your level of fitness and ability, you might be able to just show up on a random Saturday and accomplish the small-success level, as that happens often enough to be possible. To get the epic level of success, you're going to have to do a *lot* of running, training, recovery, and life-changing to make it happen.

The marathon example also illuminates the contextual nature of the levels of success. A competitive runner likely would consider the aforementioned moderate success to be just barely a small success for them. Someone who's never run before or who has a disability or injury that makes running challenging might consider the aforementioned small success an epic success.

A corollary to this is that what was once one level of success to you may be a different level of success later on in your life. For example, at one point in my life, doing twenty-five pull-ups was a small success for me; twenty additional years and about as many pounds later, twenty-five pull-ups is pushing the upper band of moderate success for me. In a similar vein, a decade ago, publishing a book would be a moderate success for me, but now it's a small success. Hitting the *New York Times* bestseller list is an epic goal—thanks for helping me get there, by the way.

Another personal example may help here. Before I understood the different levels of success, I was completely daunted by the prospect of finishing my dissertation. Success meant writing a groundbreaking dissertation that argued an interesting, original, and compelling point that would set up my later research program and earn me a position at a great university. Pressure much? But when I later considered that I could research and produce a scholarly work and I no longer needed it to get me a job or set up a later research program, it became much easier to see how I could get through it. I had unconsciously chosen an epic success as my target, but I wasn't in a place in my life where I would put epic-level effort into the project.

Our head trash—in this case, comparisitis—often clouds our judgment of the levels of success, especially when it comes to intentionally choosing small successes as our target. It's incredibly easy to fall into the trap of using other people's successes as benchmarks for our own, regardless of our desire to do what other people do to earn their level of success. We usually don't see the work other people do or have done to get to their level of success, and even when we do, we somehow think we can and should be able to catch up or take a shortcut to get there. And when we're not comparing ourselves to other people, we're comparing ourselves to some idealized version of ourselves that has it all figured out. *That* person can and would achieve greater levels of success than our current self, and we use *that* person's fictional success as a yardstick to hit ourselves with.

Here's the deal: What other people achieve is irrelevant to where you are and what level of success makes the most sense for you. That idealized version of yourself doesn't exist and what it might achieve is also irrelevant. Where you are and where you want to go is all that matters, and no one but you can choose what level of success is resonant.

The grace of the levels of success is that you can choose goal levels that align with what matters most for you. Some dimensions of your life may matter more to you than others; in those dimensions that matter less, choosing small successes makes sense. Even within a dimension, some projects and responsibilities may be less important, so you can deemphasize those with small successes, or what my friend and author Michael Bungay Stanier calls "acceptable mediocrity."[2]

Even when it comes to the idea you chose in the last chapter, you may still want to consider choosing small successes as your target. Why? Where you are in your life and career right now may be such that you know you can't commit to epic or moderate success, and it's more important to you to get some momentum and wins than to put your best work off for some day when things settle down.

What I most want to ingrain here is to match the level of success with your level of effort and commitment.

The higher the level of success, the more you'll need to do to achieve it.

Yes, it sounds obvious when stated that way, but it's far too easy for us to visualize and expect a high level of success without also committing to a high level of effort and commitment. Tying success to commitment also helps us retroactively; if we get a lower outcome than expected but also put in much lower effort than we planned, it's easier to thwart head trash about our competency because it's really about our effort.

2. Michael Bungay Stanier, *Do More Great Work: Stop the Busywork, and Start the Work That Matters* (New York: Workman, 2010).

Consider the idea you chose in the last chapter. What would each level of success look like for that idea? Considering those different levels of success and what else you have going on right now, what level of success is most resonant with you?

NO DATE = NO FINISH

A running theme throughout this chapter has been the importance of having dates assigned to goals, projects, and action steps. Simply put, if a goal, project, or action step doesn't have a date assigned to it, it's not likely to happen. Undated items get a free ticket to Someday/Maybe Land, even when they matter to you.

There are two reasons for this: (1) an undated item doesn't have any real commitment juice to it, and (2) we naturally triage items based on time requirements. These two facts are especially important when it comes to working with the people who will help us succeed—the whole reason we have the concept of dates and times is because we need a way to communicate specific times when things can and should happen.

As a simple example, consider how many "we should hang out soon!" statements actually turn into hanging out if they're not very quickly followed up with specific dates for hanging out? Consider how much more likely hanging out is if followed by "Would you like to get drinks Friday evening?" Even if Friday evening doesn't work, the specific date converts the idea into a commitment to be accepted or rejected or an alternative offered.

The same principle is at play with your goals, projects, and action items. It's also at play when you make a request of other people. Undated items are unsigned checks you can't cash.

Putting a date on an item makes it a commitment, which is one reason why some of us struggle with putting dates on items. If we can't follow through on the date, then we'll let ourselves and others down. And subconsciously we know that putting a date on something likely means we'll have to make some downstream choices to either finish or let go of an existing project since we're probably maxed out with existing projects to start with. In the moment, it's easier to put it in the someday/maybe pile; it's only when we *really* look at the pile that we realize that we're smothered by it.

The gift of dating items is that it helps us get real with displacement, and displacement channels our energy and attention. Displacement and commitment are our enemies only when we choose to ignore or downplay them. Once we honor and accept them, we can get busy doing what matters most.

When most of us think about dating items, we typically only think about due dates or completion dates. By doing this, we miss out on the grace and power of *start dates*. Yes, it's logical and obvious that every project has a discrete start date, but it's also true that many of us don't intentionally choose a start date for projects—if completion dates are slippery, start dates are doubly so.

When it comes to commitment, start dates can often be as powerful as completion dates. Start dates are analogous to the difference between being in a long-term relationship and being engaged; regardless of how long you've been together, engagement changes the relationship and requires a new way of channeling time, energy, and attention. Start and completion dates put a ring on your idea, and, yes, I'm going to invoke Queen Bey:

if you like the project (and actually want to get it done), you've got to put a ring on it.

Take a second to think about how different it feels to intentionally commit to today being the start date for your project rather than just letting it remain in Someday/Maybe Land. If you're honestly playing along, you probably felt two things simultaneously: potential movement and anxiety, as if your carefully stacked and weighted Jenga tower is about to fall over. The sense of potential movement is the future pulling you forward toward meaning making; anxiety is the present and past wanting things to stay as they are.

But remember how I said there's some grace to start dates? Think about how it feels to intentionally choose a start date of, say, three weeks from today, after you finish the current major project that's on your desk. Most people feel less anxiety but still feel that sense of movement. To avoid having your start date be a proxy for procrastination, it's important for the start date to be based on some real reason for delay. Not being emotionally ready is a poor reason; waiting until after your surgery, work trip, or move are all really good reasons, because those events count as projects.

By picking a start date, you're choosing to start directing, redirecting, and creating available time, energy, and attention toward your project. You're not committing to getting specific chunks of your project on your schedule yet, but you are committing that you *will* get those chunks scheduled.

It comes down to this: Are you starting this project today? If not today, when?

If you truly want to get it done, put a ring (date) on getting it started.

CREATE YOUR SUCCESS PACK

If you've converted your idea into a SMART goal, chosen your level of success, and put a start date on the project, you're probably beginning to feel some of the weight of the journey ahead and wondering how you're going to do it. One way you're *not* going to do it is all by yourself. That's the hard way, and if you chose an epic goal, you won't be able to do it by yourself anyway.

With your goal, level of success, and for-real start date, you have enough to start building your *success pack*. Your success pack is the group of people who are going to be instrumentally involved in helping you push your best-work project to done. Think of this group of people as the rest of the Avengers, the Fellowship of the Ring, the Sisterhood of the Traveling Pants, or the crew of the *Enterprise* (without the redshirts).

There are four kinds of people to put in your success pack:

▸ Guides ▸ Peers ▸ Supporters ▸ Beneficiaries

You'll want to include three to five people from each group for projects that you think are going to take a quarter or longer, but you may need to build a success pack for smaller projects if such projects require big changes to your habits, career, or lifestyle. If you have more people than that, you're more likely to end up a rudderless ship due to too much input and overwhelmed by having too many people to keep in the loop. Less than that in each group and you won't have enough people fuel and diverse perspectives to augment your own. Assembling three to five people per group means you'll have twelve to twenty people who have got your back, but note that a person can be in multiple groups—this is especially true for supporters and beneficiaries.

Building a team of active supporters not only gives you additional capabilities to get your project done, but it also gives some positive voices to counteract the undue attention we all give naysayers. Because of faulty wiring, we're far more likely to imagine a crowd of naysayers or see the (at most) handful of naysayers in our lives and make them the primary anchors for our fears and insecurities. It's the person who has their arms crossed while we're speaking that we latch on to, or the one out of a hundred negative comments on our work that sends us in a tailspin for days.

Rather than focus on the naysayers, we're stacking our success pack with yaysayers. Our yaysayers are the people who have seen who we are all along, been in our corner, and want and need us to succeed. Rather than trying to prove our naysayers wrong, let's prove our yaysayers right. (For many people, this refocus is both freeing and terrifying.)

Let's handle each kind of people in turn.

GUIDES

Your guides are people you look up to who have walked the road a little longer than you have. They've done more than just accomplish a certain level of success that you're after; they've done so in a way that resonates with you in terms of character and approach. Your guides serve as compasses, remote advisors, and paradigm shifters when you get stuck in seeing things in ways that aren't working for you.

Ideally your guides are alive and reachable, but you may also have some historical and larger-than-life guides that are important to you. Be careful that you humanize this latter type of guide, though, so that you don't create a model that's impossible for you to live up to. "What Would Jesus Do?" is great from an ethical perspective, but "walk on water" isn't so great when you're drowning in a project ocean.

As far as interactions go, your guides are like Yoda, Dumbledore, or Gandalf. They won't be in the work with you, they'll often give cryptic counsel that you'll struggle to understand, and they'll pop in and out randomly—and many times, when you're stuck, the way they'll pop in is with your version of "Use the force, Luke." Picking your guides is less about the *external* interactions you'll have with them than priming yourself with their worldview. Sometimes it's literally asking yourself how they would discuss your challenge or question that does all the work.

For instance, Seth Godin is one of my guides more for his character than his marketing genius. While we've had actual conversations, at this stage in my career, I disagree and argue with him in imaginary conversations multiple times per week. Our imaginary conversations are much more volatile than my imaginary conversations with Peter Drucker, Lao Tzu, Aristotle, Teddy Roosevelt, and Maya Angelou.

While historical guides aren't to be discounted, it's extremely helpful to have a few living guides in your success pack. Enrolling a living guide can be tricky, though, because it's likely that a lot of other people want their attention at the same time so that they may have no idea who you are. I'll let Pam tackle this in a sidebar since its one of her genius zones (see next page).

PEERS

Peers are people at your approximate level of accomplishment or skill who can and will regularly contribute to your project. You're likely in a reciprocal relationship where you're helping them with their projects and in regular back-and-forth communication. If your guides are in front of you, your peers are with you side by side.

When considering your peers, it's important that you don't conflate cheerleaders with yaysayers. Some of your peers should challenge your thinking and approach, as well as point out your blind spots. They're like the friends who will tell you about the salad in your teeth when you're at a party. The big difference between the unhelpful critic and the helpful critical peer is that the latter draws out the best in you rather than just making themselves look better.

PAMELA SLIM   THE PRINCIPLES OF ENROLLING A GUIDE

The most nerve-racking part of building a success pack is enrolling a guide. What is the best way to approach a very busy person who is constantly being asked for favors? Of all the people in the world who this guide could be helping, why you? Your biggest concerns are the right questions to ask and answer. Here are some guiding principles for enrolling a guide:

▸ **Equality.** A true guide is simply a more experienced equal. Your guide's body of work is deeply intertwined with your own. What kind of change in the world are they advocating? How is their mission deeply dependent on yours? Approach enrolling your guide with a focus on passion for your shared mission.

▸ **Nature.** No set of ideal guide criteria is a substitute for natural chemistry. You and your guide need to truly dig each other. Choose guides who not only have extraordinary gifts but who also share interests and values that make it fun and interesting to be together.

▸ **Commitment.** When you enroll the help of busy people, you must follow through on your commitments. Be proactive to see what kind of help they need from you. Get your work done on time.

▸ **Liberation.** My best friend Desireé Adaway describes the quality of great relationships as "liberatory." It's your job to keep your relationship with your guide free of expectation. Where freedom exists, connection grows.

Pamela Slim is an author, community builder, and business coach. She focused her first decade in business consulting with large companies such as HP, Charles Schwab, and Chevron. The second decade has been focused on helping entrepreneurs thrive in the new world of work through her coaching and books *Escape from Cubicle Nation: From Corporate Prisoner to Thriving Entrepreneur*, and *Body of Work: Finding the Thread That Ties Your Story Together*.

It's also important to make sure you have some peers who are outside of your discipline, field, or echo chamber. Few things will propel your work more than having a successful peer who isn't deeply familiar with your discipline, field, or work, because they'll ask the questions you've forgotten are questions, and you won't dismiss them as beneath your consideration or as something coming from a critic. The other major upshot to having a peer outside of your field, discipline, or industry is that they'll have a lot of insights and analogies from *their* discipline and field that will cross-pollinate your work.

SUPPORTERS

Your supporters are the people who are doing work with and for you to help you get the project done. More so than status or level of accomplishment, you can ask the people in this category for support and expect them to meet reasonable deadlines—guides and peers are much more removed from this aspect.

Your most important supporters often are outside of the office. For instance, your spouse or partner may be a key supporter, or would be if you actively enrolled them to support your project. In a similar vein, it may be the neighborhood kids who tend your lawn on Saturdays and babysit in the evenings so you get in some extra project time. Or maybe it's your roommate who does most of the grocery shopping, cooking, and dishes while you're on a deadline.

Actively building and curating your support team is the single most important practice that you can do to ensure that you're finishing your best work. Your support team is your force multiplier—no matter how competent you are, you'll always be constrained by the amount of functional hours you have available in a day.

In addition, few joys are as sublime as winning as a team; at root, we're cooperative animals who are biochemically rewarded for cooperative success. We were made to slay dragons *together*.

In theory, building a good support team isn't that difficult. In practice, it's much harder because most people have to work through a lot of head trash around asking for help and claiming that their work is important enough to prioritize. Women especially struggle with these challenges because we socialize women to be supporters and to be asked, but it's rare that people will ask you to do your best work and to pick themselves to support *your* best work. Men struggle more due to the self-made-man myth and the mindset that asking for help and support makes them weak.

I'm well aware that I've juxtaposed the reality that we're naturally cooperative creatures and we have a lot of head trash that keeps us from collaborating. There's no logical tension there, but it's an experiential tension that plays out every day. Furthermore, the tension between cooperation and independence plays out in every dimension of our lives from our relationships to politics, so why would we think it wouldn't play out in our best work as well?

BENEFICIARIES

Your beneficiaries are the specific people who will benefit from the completion of your work. Whether it's full bellies, full minds, or full hearts, your beneficiaries' lives will be better because of the work you've done.

There's an important corollary here: If you *don't* finish your best work, your beneficiaries will be worse off.

Whatever pain your work heals or delight it delivers won't be healed or delivered without you doing your work, and there's no substitute for your best work because no one else will create what you create in the way that you create it.

I state the corollary because it's been my experience that it can be helpful when your project gets hard or you're stuck in the void. It's one thing when your best work is just about you and what you want to do; it's quite another when you think about the people who will be worse off if you don't stand tall, lean into thrashing, and work your way to done. This is where the "specific" piece of the definition of beneficiaries comes into play, for there's a big difference between an imaginary person being worse off and some specific person you know. You might quit on yourself; few of us will quit on other people.

An additional reason beneficiaries need to be specific people that you know is so you can ask them for feedback about what you're building. Your head trash, ignorance, and arrogance can keep you stuck and take you way off course; having the courage to show your work and ask your beneficiaries how it's landing can keep you on course and inspire you to finish it up.

DON'T JUST BUILD YOUR SUCCESS PACK — USE IT

While it can be fun to think about who might be in your success pack, the real magic happens when you make a plan for how you'll actively use it. Sure, you may have one of your trusted peers in your success pack, but how are you going to do your best work with them? How frequently will you be in contact with them? About what? And what will you need to show them so that they can provide their best feedback?

Here are the steps to go from idea to action on this strategy:

1 **List the three to five people who are a part of each group.** Remember that you're looking for *specific* people—"single moms in Idaho" don't count as a beneficiary, for example. In this step, you're building your phone-a-friend list.

2 **For each person, brainstorm at least three specific ways they can help you or you can help them.** If you can't think of at least three items, you likely have the wrong person on the list or don't know the person well enough. For your guides, perhaps list what types of questions you would like to ask them or who they may be able to introduce you to. For peers, list skills, connections, or perspectives they bring to bear. For supporters, list what work they can do to help you do yours. For beneficiaries, list what questions would reveal whether what you're doing is actually making their world better. Now you know what to phone your friends about.

3 **Determine the frequency of communication that would be most supportive for you and the project.** For a default, consider a monthly pulse for your peers and beneficiaries and an at-least-weekly pulse for your supporters; guides are more as-needed and will often find you.

4 **Let each person know they're a part of your success pack.** Given that it's unlikely they know what a success pack is, just let them know you're working on something and you would love their help. Based on your answers to questions 2 and 3, communicate to them how they can help and about how much you'll be in touch with them, so they know what they're agreeing to and what to expect from you. Guides are trickier because you may not be able to enroll them due to their being out of reach or no longer alive; even when they're alive, the most you might want to do is email them and let them know they're an inspiration for the project you're working on. If you have a mentor relationship with your guide, then you can enroll them as if they were a peer.

5 **Proactively communicate with and show your work to them per the pulse established above.** It's not the job of your guides, peers, and beneficiaries to follow up with you and ask how you're doing; it's your job to keep them informed and engaged. The exception here is if your guides and peers agree to help keep you accountable, in which case it may be their jobs to follow up with you if they don't hear from you on the pulse you jointly agreed to.

It's the fourth step that terrifies people, because assembling your success pack makes things *real* really fast. Suddenly there are twelve to twenty people who care about you, who can help you, and who expect something from you. Suddenly you've got skin in the game, deadlines, and accountability partners. Suddenly your excuses, procrastination, and what-abouts morph into a simple "Will you or won't you?"

Of course, in that same step, you've set yourself up such that completion is nearly inevitable as long as you show up. So if you're ready to make the completion of your project nearly inevitable, work through the steps.

If you're ready to start finishing your best work, take your idea from the previous chapter and work it through the steps in this chapter. You'll probably need a two-hour block to work through converting your idea into a SMART goal, choosing your level of success, picking a date for the project, and brainstorming who's in your success pack. You'll probably need another two-hour block to contact most of the people in your success pack, depending on how long you thrash.

At this point, it comes down to whether you're willing to put a ring on this project and build your team. Your natural inclination will be to get ready and then commit, but I'm asking you to do the opposite: commit *so that you* get ready. Without the commitment, it's unlikely that you're going to make space in the world to do your project—that's what we're turning to next.

CHAPTER 4 TAKEAWAYS

▶ A SMART goal is simple, meaningful, actionable, realistic, and trackable.

▶ The three levels of success—small, moderate, and epic—require a corresponding amount of effort and focus, and you can't do everything at the epic level.

▶ If a project doesn't have start and completion dates, it's not likely that it's going to get done.

▶ Your success pack consists of four kinds of people: guides, peers, supporters, and beneficiaries.

▶ Activating your success pack makes your project real because others get invested in your goal and you've made your first real commitment.

You will never find time for anything.
If you want time, you must make it.
CHARLES BUXTON, *Notes of Thought*

MAKE SPACE FOR YOUR PROJECT

Up until now, you've been making space in your mind and heart to start doing your best work. While it's natural to think the next step is to jump right into the project—or, if you're the "look before you leap" type, to start planning the project—you're going to very quickly confront the reality that there's nowhere in your schedule for the project to go. You would only be adding more to an overfull plate, and it would only continue to add to your creative constipation.

You need to make a wedge for your project first. The principle here is that if you make space for one best-work project, you'll have the satisfaction and momentum to reuse that space for the next project and likely be able to create additional space for an additional project. Over time, you'll find that more of your days are spent doing your best work. Or at least you'll be able to see that amid all the work that doesn't call to you, you're able to make progress on stuff that matters most to you.

The challenge is that time is surprisingly hard for us to think about, and most of the ways we *do* think about time don't work for us. While we're rethinking work, we'll also need to rethink time. Throughout this chapter I'll be using time and space interchangeably because it turns out that we're better at understanding spatial metaphors, and using these metaphors makes us better at prioritizing the work we're going to be doing. Along the same vein, I'm going to be tying work to time/space because work only happens through time.

Because thinking about time is so hard to do, let's take it one chunk at a time.

CHUNKING, LINKING, AND SEQUENCING: THE THREE ESSENTIAL SKILLS TO BENDING TIME

Thinking about time in general terms can be interesting, but it's not very useful or practical unless you happen to be a philosopher or physicist. To make time relevant, it's typically better to tie it to a particular context. Since our context is work, we'll be using that as our anchor to avoid getting swept away in the multiverse.

Recall that we don't work on ideas; we work on projects. More specifically, we don't work on projects; we work on chunks of projects linked together in the right sequence. *Chunking*, *linking*, and *sequencing* thus become the simple concepts that will be the Swiss Army knife of this chapter.

Even though the concepts are simple to understand, let's define these key concepts:

▶ **Chunking.** Splitting projects into coherent, doable parts.

▶ **Linking.** Joining chunks together so that they hang together.

▶ **Sequencing.** Linking chunks together into a logical order in space and time.

The simplest expression of a chunk is a verb-noun construct because it tells you the action that's being taken on something. So *book*, *closet*, and *John* aren't chunks because they're just nouns; *read book*, *clean closet*, and *email John* are chunks. Much like making a non-SMART goal something you can't abide seeing, I want nouns without verbs on your action lists to be something that you'll forever be unable to tolerate without fixing.

Let's use building blocks as a way to illustrate project building. Each individual block is a chunk of a project. The tops and bottoms of standard building blocks are the way we link the chunks. The order we place and link the blocks is the sequence.

To continue with this example, at some point in your life—and I'm not judging if it was earlier today—you've started sticking random blocks together with no clear idea of what you were building. That's analogous to lacking a SMART goal. You may have had an idea of what you wanted to build but hadn't thought through how you were going to do it—you didn't have a plan.

If you've ever played with any kind of building block system, you already know how to chunk, link, and sequence time and projects. Now would be a particularly good time to thank your parents and teachers. (Okay, wait until you finish this section.)

Time, however, is conceptually slippery; we could divide time up into any number of segments that we wanted to because the endless stream of time has no natural division. This very slipperiness is why humanity made conventions such as seconds, minutes, and months; without those conventions, time is relative to the speaker's particular use in that moment. We can tie the sizes of our chunks to the standard divisions of time we already use. Thus we end up with year-sized chunks, (annual) quarter-sized chunks, month-sized chunks, week-sized chunks, day-sized chunks, hour-sized chunks, minute-sized chunks, and second-sized chunks.

The reality is, though, that some of those *logical* chunks are terrible chunks to use to plan (for most of us) because they don't match our experience and reality. Ironically, it's the *smaller* chunks of time that are the slipperiest for us. We can't mark seconds, minutes, hours, and days very well, yet those are the chunks of time that most time-management systems and many of our practices try to get us to use. Given that we've only been measuring in seconds, minutes, and hours for the last few hundred years, that's understandable. Just because you put an organic being in a factory doesn't mean that it becomes a machine.

So rather than try to use all the logical chunks, we're going to focus on year-, quarter-, month-, week-, two-hour-, and fifteen-minute-sized chunks. Before we jump into using the bigger chunks of time, let's pause to discuss the two-hour- and fifteen-minute-sized chunks, since we'll be using them the most.

After working with thousands of people, I've experienced that most people have a good idea of how many fifteen-minute or two-hour chunks it will take to get a project done, if I ask them to think in terms of such blocks. But if I ask them how many minutes or hours something will take, they have no idea what to say. Two-hour- and fifteen-minute-sized chunks are thus powerful anchors because they better track our natural attentional and habitual cycles. For convention, I'll call a chunk of work that can be done in fifteen minutes a *task* and a chunk that can be done in two hours a *block*.

Try it. Think about an item on today's to-do list. Does it seem like it's going to be a fifteen-minute task (or two) or a two-hour block?

An important assumption that I'm baking into my chunks is the cost of context- and mental-switching that is often discounted. Many people balk when I suggest assigning a fifteen-minute chunk to composing each email message response, but they're not counting the three-minute cognitive reset that happens between each email. Ten minutes isn't long enough to adequately process the email message, but longer than twenty minutes is too long. (This accounts for why so many people are drowned in email and why it takes up so much of their day. Reading, thinking through, responding to, or composing twelve important emails would take the majority of a standard work morning or afternoon.) Fifteen minutes is thus the Goldilocks time assignment for each email.

Similarly, thirty minutes or an hour rarely feels long enough to get into, tussle with, complete, and exit from high-level analytical, synthetic, or creative work. Two hours is a better chunk, as it allows us to do all of the above, walk around, go to the bathroom, refresh our coffee, and so on, all while remaining ostensibly focused.

While the discussion above has been on the minimum size of an engagement threshold, the task and block conventions also help us with the *maximum* amount of time we can be fruitfully engaged in a chunk. Think about your emotional experience and active engagement on an email or admin call on which you spent longer than fifteen minutes. Think about what happened to your attention, focus, energy, and momentum on high-level work after two hours. In both cases there's an upper limit to how long we can remain fruitfully engaged before we experience emotional or cognitive deterioration. It's a cruel irony that most of us want to do *more* high-level work *longer* and do as little of the admin work as possible, but the work on our plate is high on admin and seemingly low on high-level work.

A further reflection would yield a similar minimum-maximum engagement period for the other chunk sizes as well. Even though we tend to underestimate how long something will take, we also know when a quarter-sized chunk has dragged into too many quarters and years. We also know when a week-sized chunk has fallen into too many weeks and months.

THE PROJECT PYRAMID

The *project pyramid* builds on chunking, linking, and sequencing because it shows how bigger projects contain smaller projects, as well as how smaller chunks tie together to build momentum. It helps us see, at the same time, the wall (best work) *and* the bricks (smaller chunks) that make up the wall. We're going to get a lot of mileage out of the project pyramid, but I'm going to be up front that it can be conceptually challenging to understand and emotionally hard to accept. Shifting timescales is hard for all of us to do, but it's easier than accepting the reality of how much we've committed to.

Some projects are really big and will require a lot of time and subprojects (chunks) to complete. Publishing a book, starting a new business, completing a major work initiative, getting a degree, and moving across the country are examples of big projects that will take many years or quarters to complete.

Other projects can be done in a day or a week. Volunteering at the bake sale, getting your kids sorted for the first week of school, completing the weekly quality assurance report, and organizing the Closet of Doom are examples of smaller projects that can be done in a day or a week.

Simple stuff, I know. The challenge is that we often set goals for ourselves that convert into large projects that themselves contain subprojects, without seeing the collective weight of those projects, especially as you go further down in timescale.

Take a simple (but very unrealistic) model in which a yearlong project has four quarter-sized chunks (for the year), every quarter-sized chunk has three month-sized chunks, every month has four week-sized chunks, and every week-sized chunk has five two-hour chunks (for that project), and each work block contains eight fifteen-minute chunks. One annual objective would spawn 1,920 tasks. Those 1,920 tasks convert into three full work months of time (assuming forty hours per week and four weeks per work month) if someone worked on only that project without wait time and interruption.

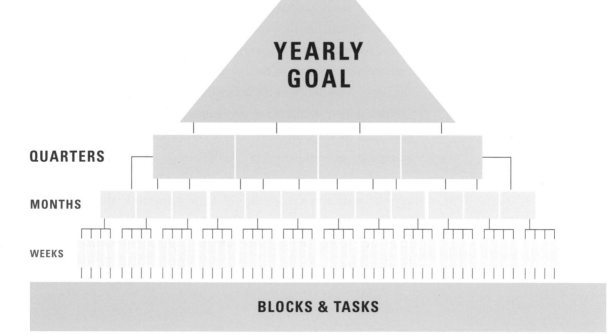

You can now see why I call it the project *pyramid*. One large project spawns many subprojects at lower levels.

The unrealistic part of the model is that it's too uniform *and* that higher-level chunks usually contain more concurrent lower-level chunks than above. The three-work-months estimate above is thus too low.

Let that sink in for a minute. The simple model that turned one yearlong project into three full work months is an *underestimate* of what it would take to see one year-sized project through.

So the person that rolls into the year with seven goals that will require year-sized projects has started a game they're *very* unlikely to win. You've no doubt heard some version of the maxim to have no more than one, three, or five (depending on who's talking) ambitious goals (objectives) if you actually want to get them done; the project pyramid underpins why doing fewer projects isn't a nice-to-consider maxim but a necessary practice if you're serious about doing your best work.

When people really see how an annual goal, chunked down, leads to this much bottom-level work, it can be the emotional equivalent of the Ice Bucket Challenge. It explains the too-full to-do list and the feelings of overwhelm and creative undertow that so many people experience. People have told me that, for years, they've just assumed they weren't productive or couldn't get it together.

The reality is that they've been trying to put twenty-two units of stuff into a ten-unit bag. Time is currently the ultimate constraint—we can't bend it, expand it, manage it, or alter it. We can only account for it and work within the constraint.

If you're now feeling the weight of the overfull project load you've been carrying, pause and take a breath. Now that you see it, you can start to get real about removing all the excess weight that's only making it harder for you to thrive and do your best work. At the same time, it will help you make better choices going forward. This is another one of those places where displacement is your friend.

HOW COMMON PROJECT WORDS TIE TOGETHER

I had a braingasm a decade and a half ago when I synthesized two simple observations: (1) verbs often give an indication to how big a chunk of work is, and (2) certain verbs follow and contain others. It sounds hyperbolic, but my planning world was forever leveled up from that day forward, and I sincerely hope yours will be the same if you're just coming upon this synthesis. (This braingasm is what led to the pyramid after years of figuring out how to articulate it.)

Some chunks will naturally go *with* others, and some chunks go *in* others. When we articulate chunks as verb-noun constructs, we see that the verb gives us an idea of the size of the work and the noun stays constant throughout the project.

Take "Hire Skyler" as a project. Throughout the project, the verb sequence might be Research ▸ Email (to Schedule) ▸ Interview ▸ Evaluate ▸ Decide On ▸ Hire. Bonus points if you see that that sequence of verbs is a repeatable sequence and thus a standard workflow.

But wait, there's more! We use some common verbs across the world of work because, as a species, we've needed some conventions for the same reasons we've needed time conventions.

Here are some conventional verbs as well as what size of a chunk they relate to:

▷ Quarter- or month-sized project verbs (for work that needs a few week- or month-sized projects to complete):
  ▪ Rework
  ▪ Develop
  ▪ Strategize
  ▪ Launch/Ship
  ▪ Build
  ▪ Publish (books, articles)
  ▪ Kick off
  ▪ Move/Relocate

▷ Week-sized project verbs (for work that needs at least one block, but probably not more than five for each coherent segment of work):
  ▪ Research
  ▪ Decide on
  ▪ Collaborate with
  ▪ Create
  ▪ Plan
  ▪ Design
  ▪ Analyze/evaluate
  ▪ Coordinate
  ▪ Promote
  ▪ Edit
  ▪ Apply

▷ Task verbs (for work that can be done in fifteen minutes):
  ▪ Email
  ▪ Call
  ▪ Sort
  ▪ Read
  ▪ Send
  ▪ Check
  ▪ Review
  ▪ Find
  ▪ Compile
  ▪ Schedule
  ▪ Make
  ▪ Text
  ▪ Fax
  ▪ Mail
  ▪ Print

The list above isn't meant to be exhaustive, but it provides a universal list that applies across industries, professions, and contexts and thus serves as the Rosetta stone for chunking and planning. Feel free to add verbs that are specific and common to your context too. (It's telling that jargon is usually nouns, not verbs.)

So you can see how this works, the following are five common, simplified chunk sequences for some of the bigger projects I mentioned in the last section:

- **Moving to a new city.** Research places, decide on places, plan moving schedule, sell or get rid of stuff, pack stuff, move stuff, unpack stuff.

- **Starting a new business.** Research business ideas, decide on model, make a business plan, design product, create product, promote product, deliver product.

- **Publishing a book.** Brainstorm book ideas, decide on book idea, create an outline, draft manuscript, collaborate with editor/readers, edit manuscript, create marketing plan, promote book.

- **Getting a degree.** Evaluate degree options, decide on degree options, research universities to apply to, decide on universities to apply to, apply to universities, evaluate university offers, plan move to university, move to university, collaborate with advisor on course schedule, decide on courses, and take courses. Rinse and repeat the last three chunks for a few years.

- **Developing a fundraiser.** Evaluate fundraising needs, decide on fundraising strategy, plan fundraising campaign, coordinate with fundraisers, promote campaign.

See how we could take almost any project and do this? It's not that strategists and planners like myself are supersmart but rather we've internalized a small set of verbs and how they relate.

Also notice how each of the chunks I listed actually have parts in them that I didn't spell out; someone with familiarity with that type of project would know how to do the chunking. This again highlights the power of success packs. When you're assembling them, you can pick people who have done projects similar to what you're planning and they can help you with your chunking.

A big missing piece, of course, is how long each chunk will take. We'll go into more detail about how to figure that out in the next chapter when we discuss how to plan a specific project. Our purpose here is to get you to see how much space a project will need and how to go about creating space for it.

THE FIVE PROJECTS RULE

I just pulled a rabbit out of a hat, and you either noticed it or you're frustrated because something's missing. What makes the trick work is that I constrained the timescale, which let me not worry too much about the details and specifics that are relevant to the lower timescales.

As we consider bigger timescales, it's important to alter the level of specificity when it comes to thinking about action. When you're thinking about the forest (time), focusing on the leaves (action) short-circuits your ability to consider either the forest or leaves. Each shift in timescale is thus a shift in perspective.

People often struggle with visualization, planning, and reviewing because they slip between perspectives too fluidly. For instance, when you're at the monthly perspective, the quarterly perspective informs the *why* of the month and the weekly perspective informs the *how* of the month. That general rule follows for all timescales:

when you need clarity of purpose, shift up;
when you need clarity of action steps, shift down.

Constraining the timescale is the only real way we can make sense of everything we're carrying because we can't process more than one time perspective at a time. It's the cognitive equivalent of trying to look simultaneously at a piece of paper that's six inches from you and something that's a mile away.

Thus enters the "No More Than Five Active Projects Per Timescale" rule, which we'll shorthand to the *Five Projects*

Rule because the former is too unwieldy. Let's unpack "no more than five" and "active projects" separately.

Concerning "no more than five," decades of research, observation, and experimentation have shown me that most people won't complete more than five total projects per timescale. Since how many projects we *finish* is more important than how many we *start*, we do ourselves no favors by committing to more projects than we'll be able to do. In reality, three projects is a better limit for creative and/or professional projects because it leaves bandwidth to use for life/personal projects and accounts for the work we're doing but not counting.

"Active projects" makes you commit to projects that you're actively pushing forward as opposed to those that you're just thinking about, queued for the future, or are hanging on to but aren't actually doing anything with. Your active projects are the ones that are on your metaphorical desktop.

The Five Projects Rule is simple to understand but may be incredibly difficult to practice, especially if you limit yourself to three projects to account for personal and undercounted work. But remember the project pyramid: your three or five projects may contain subprojects, depending on the time perspective.

What the Five Projects Rule allows us to do is check our commitments and do routine planning quickly. For instance, if you're doing your weekly planning, you don't need to get into the nitty-gritty of each day—you can just focus on the five projects you're doing this week. If you've done your monthly planning and picked your five projects for the month, the week's projects should be chunks of one or more of those monthly projects. As I said, timescale constraining and the project pyramid do a lot of the work for you.

To give an example of how this works, I'll share a snapshot of my five projects for the current month, week, and day.

August 2018

1. Draft chapters for *Start Finishing*
2. Launch the 2019 momentum planners
3. Present at Camp GLP (Good Life Project)

This Week

1. Draft chapter 6 of *Start Finishing*
2. Prepare workshop for Camp GLP
3. Attend Camp GLP
4. Finish proposal for event in March 2019

Today

1. Draft chapter 6 of *Start Finishing*
2. Finish proposal for event in March 2019
3. Meet with client at 1:00 p.m.

Given that the deadline for this book is in October and how many of my available blocks it's taking—which isn't a complaint, because I love writing—I know not to add anything more than what's already active. I'm also intentionally not doing a lot of month- and week-sized projects on the personal side.

At the weekly level, I don't have to specify more than what I've done above. Fixed times for events such as flights and meetings are on my calendar and I know when those are, so I don't need to include them in my weekly planning. But preparing for my workshop and attending Camp GLP are two different projects, and the latter prevents me from doing anything else starting Wednesday—I don't work well on planes, and when I'm at an event, I try to do nothing more than be fully present and connect with people.

At the daily level, I don't need to specify when I'm doing the work because that's driven by my week block schedule. I know I'm going to be writing in the morning, meeting with my client from my office, and, after that, completing the proposal for the event from my office. I also have some admin tasks to do that are batched in that admin block that I don't need to specify because they're captured in my work management software.

When I sit down to make next week's plan, I only need to update my weekly plan and go from there. You can probably guess what next week looks like, given how the projects are linked.

What's not included above is the fact that I have a full roster of clients on top of the creative work that I do. I've learned to not give myself five project slots at the monthly level when my client schedule is full because, though it's unlikely that I would be creating during those times, holding all of those worlds, attending meetings, and doing prep work displaces my ability to do another monthly level project. I could just as easily write down "serve clients" as a monthly slot, but I don't need to at this point because I know it's there. Simplicity favors removing the slot and not writing it, and, as long as I stick with limiting the number of projects I commit to in the future, it works. (It took me a few years to learn to assume I'd be fully booked in the future too.)

My service work actually falls under the category of recurring projects. Like personal projects, they're often undercounted. If you're being truthful about what your days, weeks, and months look like, you may see that 50 to 75 percent of your available time, energy, and attention is already committed to recurring stuff. If that's the case, you may only be able to give yourself one or two project slots to commit to; this may also mean you need to communicate and negotiate with your boss about the never-ending stream of projects they want to give you every day. Recurring projects and tasks are some of the first things to start delegating to other people. As a general rule, if you can list the steps it takes to do something, you can delegate all or major parts of the work to someone else.

A major upshot of the Five Projects Rule is that it allows you to work from a smaller, more focused list of action items rather than trying to decode and parse the To-Do List of Doom that so many people create for themselves. Capturing and dumping action items is one activity with its own space; the Five Projects Rule is the output of processing those action items. Trying to drive your momentum from your dumping ground is like having to dig through laundry baskets every time you need to dress, without knowing which laundry basket is clean and which is dirty. Sure, you can do it, but you're setting yourself up for crazy-making and unwelcome surprises.

Aside from illustrating the magic of timescale constraining, I wanted to show how the project pyramid works with quarter-sized projects because

mastering quarter-sized projects is the secret sauce of doing your best work.

To return to the air sandwich, linking finished quarter-sized projects is what positively fills the gap between the big stuff and day-to-day stuff. The Five Projects Rule helps us overcome the challenges of having no realistic plan and too few resources because, once we accept the constraint, we're able to use what we have to create a plan that will actually work.

CONVERT YOUR WEEKLY SCHEDULE INTO COHERENT BLOCKS

The last major stop on the space-making bus before you jump into actually planning out your best-work project is to zoom down and constrain your focus to the weekly perspective. Since work happens in blocks, if there are no open blocks in which to put your project—or you don't use the blocks when you put your project there—you're not going to get any momentum on your project. When you *do* use those blocks, you'll have the satisfaction of making progress on your best work. The weekly perspective is also the longest level of perspective that people feel comfortable shaping and planning.

Another reason the weekly perspective is so powerful is because it's the level where people really see the standing constraints that are already on their schedule. Between commutes, meetings at work, places the kids need to be, recurring community meetings and events, trash pickup days, and the various logistics of everyday life, most of us can clearly see that we're not starting a new day from a clean slate. All of that disappears at the monthly perspective, and the daily perspective doesn't show us the pattern well enough for us to override the magical thinking that the stuff on today's schedule is a one-off thing.

The weekly perspective is thus the perfect level for us to start rebuilding our schedules such that they go from looking like Swiss cheese, with random holes and chunks, to more coherent and purposeful blocks that support us doing our best work.

At the weekly perspective, there are four basic blocks that we can build into our days:

▸ **Focus blocks.** 90–120-minute blocks of time when we're especially creative, inspired, and able to do high-level work that requires focus.

▸ **Social blocks.** 90–120-minute blocks of time when we're primed and energetically in the right space to meet other people.

▸ **Admin blocks.** 30–60-minute lower-energy blocks of time when we're not in the zone to do the work that requires heavy lifting but there are still other types of work we can do effectively.

▸ **Recovery blocks.** Variable-length blocks of time that we use for activities that recharge us, such as exercise, meditation, self-care, and intentional idling.

The time ranges above account for transition, bathroom breaks, refilling drinks, and so on. A single-focus block may contain a few breaks for stretching, walking, rumination, bathroom, coffee refills, and so on, as long as we don't switch our focus and context to something else. It can also include whatever project review, outlining, and work wrap-up that we do while working on that project.

Let's walk through each of these blocks in more detail so you can see where they fit on your weekly schedule.

FOCUS BLOCKS

I've got good news and bad news when it comes to focus blocks. The bad news is that most people have a hard time creating and using more than three per day because of distractions, interruptions, daily routines, and a lack of intention. The good news is that you can get a lot done with three focus blocks per day, and accepting the constraint will make your life a lot easier and happier.

Okay, there's another bit of bad news: my experience working with and teaching thousands of people shows that most people don't have a free focus block to work on the projects they most want to. Their schedules look more like Swiss cheese, and they're trying to do their creative work *after* they've done other kinds of work either all day long or first thing. This is what leads to the cruel irony I mentioned earlier, wherein they don't get to do as much of the work they want to do because they have a lot more of the work they don't want to do.

Focus blocks fuel your best work. No or too few focus blocks equals no finished best work. It's really that simple.

Focus blocks are 90 to 120 minutes to tap into the way we natively understand segments of time as mentioned above. They become the atomic unit to use for your projects as well. Anything over ten hours starts to become hard for us to deal with because it gets amorphous and hard to visualize; five focus blocks is easier to understand because we can visualize the chunks of the projects we can do in that amount of time.

If you've ever put off doing a "bigger" creative project because you simply didn't know how to get started or how much time it would take, you already know what I'm talking about. Spending twenty creative hours on a project over the course of a month feels overwhelming, but working on that project for a creative block a day doesn't. Mathematically, it may be the same amount of work, but motivationally it feels different to a lot of people.

Though most people top out at three focus blocks per day, it's quite common for people to go on creative sprints, retreats, or pushes wherein they push over that limit. The usual result is that they'll be depleted and sluggish for the next few days and wonder what's wrong. This would be like working out for four hours when you normally work out for one hour. You would expect to be sore and/or fatigued the next day, even if you really enjoyed the workout. The same is true for going on a focus-block sprint. Consistent progress is better than fits and starts.

The number of focus blocks you have available is the limiting factor to how quickly and steadily you'll be able to make progress on your best-work projects. Many people misdiagnose their struggles with getting their best work done as procrastination, lack of capability, or lack of creativity, when the root cause is they just don't have any or enough focus blocks in their schedule to get started and keep going. It's not a lack of discipline but rather a lack of boundaries and intention.

SOCIAL BLOCKS

For many people, focus blocks and admin blocks can be summed up as "the work I want to do" and "the work I don't want to do," respectively. A social block is simply a block of time used for interacting with others in real time. We tend to favor social blocks over admin blocks, even for introverts, but their purpose is different than focus blocks. Focus blocks are focused on *creating* something whereas social blocks are focused on *connecting with* someone.

Real-time collaboration, brainstorming, and thought partnering with someone else creates a hybrid block, and it requires individual creative and social energy as well as cocreative energy. Most people find it better to group them as a social block, though, because most projects require solo focus blocks to get done, and collaborative social blocks often spawn work that needs to be done during a (solo) focus block.

It's important to discuss the different purposes of social blocks because people often discount their value by saying they "didn't get anything done" with them. The time you spend with your friends, family, colleagues, success pack, and tribe is valuable. Sure, it displaces other kinds of work, but that doesn't mean it's less valuable than other work, especially when you consider how lonely and disconnected creative people are (as a whole).

If there's a part of your work that requires you to spend real time with people, that part of your work goes in social blocks. For that reason I sometimes use social blocks and service blocks interchangeably to remind people that real-time service hours are social blocks.

Aside from the intrinsic value of social blocks, they make for great bookends to other blocks because most of us honor commitments to other people more than we honor commitments to ourselves. When we're in the flow, it's easy for us to bleed a focus block into the next block of time, sometimes to our own detriment in the following days when we're creatively winded. Similarly, sandwiching an admin block between two social blocks creates a coherent flow for both because there's often some type of admin work that follows social blocks.

ADMIN BLOCKS

Your particular context will determine what counts as admin work, but in general, email, phone calls, digital/paper filing, low-level editing, bookkeeping, organizing your projects—whether that's cleaning up brushes, scrubbing code, reviewing and making to-do lists, formatting documents, or updating your task management system—and anything that supports your best work but isn't your best work itself, counts as an admin block.

That broad list of work may be exactly the type of stuff you don't want to do—what I call frogs, from a quip from Mark Twain, and, yes, we'll come back to frogs later—but it still needs to get done. Not doing the admin work catches up with you somewhere down the road.

That said, many people find that once they start using their focus blocks well, admin blocks are far more tolerable and sometimes even enjoyable for several reasons:

▸ Admin blocks give you time to reflect upon your work, and they create space and context for things to gel.

▸ Knowing that there will be admin blocks allows you to stress less about all the admin work that needs to be attended to. There's a time and space for everything.

▸ Well-positioned admin blocks make it easier to catch the frogs because those tasks are confined to smaller periods of the day.

Imagine that you've already had a day where you've "left it all on the field" when it comes to how you spent your focus blocks, and you're in the sweet spot of both spent and satisfied. And *then* you get to tackle some of the other important work that's been building up. It's a double win.

But all too often the reverse of the double win happens, in that we start and spend our days rolling from admin block to admin block until we don't have the mojo or time left to fuel a focus block. Sometimes we feel as if we need to attend to the admin work that too often comes swaddled in urgent packaging, and once we're done with that, we can do our best work. But admin work trickles in as fast as we can get it done and thus we rarely get "done" with it enough for us to do our best work.

If you're getting further ahead on your admin work but getting further behind on your best work, you're either going the wrong way or you aren't honoring that the admin work ties into deeper values and goals that are more important to you than your best work.

You might wonder why admin blocks are thirty to sixty minutes when I've previously stated that fifteen minutes is a coherent chunk of time for us. This comes down to motivation, engagement thresholds, and planning. Most people are more motivated from having a few items checked off rather than just one. Regarding engagement thresholds, once you've shifted context into doing admin work, it makes sense to stay there for a bit rather than switching to a different context. And for planning, it's too unwieldy to plan for fifteen minutes at a time.

Thus in admin blocks you *batch* admin tasks together. Batching work is simply lumping the same kind of work together—for instance, making all your admin calls in a block or processing similar kinds of emails—so that you stay in that context and flow. We'll come back to batching later because it's one of the simplest ways to keep momentum and efficiently use your time.

RECOVERY BLOCKS

Focus, social, and admin blocks are energy *output* blocks, and just like a battery that outputs energy, they need to be recharged. While it might seem as if we don't need to be intentional about our recovery blocks, I've learned the hard way that we actually need to be *more* intentional about them than about any of the other blocks precisely because we're overfocused on output. Most of us put the other three in the "productive and valuable" bucket, but it's the recovery blocks that allow us to do that work.

Recovery blocks do more than allow us to be mindful as we do our work. If there's anything that will keep us from doing our best work, it's poor health, illness, and pain. Recovery blocks keep those at bay. Anyone who's worked through health challenges, illness, injuries, and pain has dealt with the frustrating reality that recovery blocks displace everything else. I spent five of the ten months I had to write this book dealing with a painful condition that eventually required minor surgery; five months of losing at least a focus block a day doesn't help a writer stay on his timeline.

Each of us has different activities that help us recover and recharge. Extroverts might like to go to a party, whereas introverts might want to curl up with their pet and a book. Yoga might do it for some, whereas CrossFit might do it for others. What's more important than the type of activity is what the activity does for you.

Acknowledging and using recovery blocks allows you to find dead zones in your day that can be repurposed for recovery. For instance, I'm usually spent on the creative, admin, and social fronts around 4:30 p.m. and rarely hit a groove again until 6:30 p.m. Doing anything that requires using my brain during that time amounts to a lot of clicking and mindless grazing, so I'm far better off when I designate that time as a recovery block.

A much as social blocks make for great bookends to focus blocks, recovery blocks can also be a good follow-up to a focus block since focus blocks are often the most taxing. While your mind is recharging and recycling, you can be doing something else.

As a general rule, plan on a recovery block for every two focus or social blocks.

DO YOU NEED TO RENAME SOME BLOCKS?

The four blocks I've mentioned are universal templates that account for, well, everything. For instance, sleeping is a recovery block, as is eating, bathing, and so on. Unless you need to be more intentional about your sleeping, it's not particularly useful to put sleeping on your weekly schedule.

But many people wonder where to put things such as childcare, cooking, chores, commuting, and so on. They're closest to admin work or social time, so I'd put them in admin or social blocks as appropriate.

Designating chores as admin blocks may not do it for you, and you might balk at the idea of *just* connecting with your kids rather than doing that *and* chores at the same time. So maybe you want something like a chore block or a family block.

While there are some downsides to trying to stuff too many kinds of activities into one block of time, watching TV with your roommate while you're doing laundry and talking to your mom might really work for you. What doesn't work for a lot of people is having too many kinds of blocks, as it adds too many kinds of things to juggle all over again and that's precisely what we're trying to avoid.

I'm also aware that it's a foreign or anathematic idea to apply work-centric frameworks in our personal lives. There's a lot of value and clarity that comes from "making it all work" in the sense that there's no real difference in the way we value, prioritize, plan, and spend our personal time and our work time, especially because people too often underprioritize their personal lives and overprioritize their work lives. But if using blocking categories in your personal life is so dissonant that you'll reject the whole framework, then don't use the blocking principles at home. Thus you probably won't need any more than the four blocks I've discussed above. (But you still need recovery blocks at work!)

THREE FOCUS BLOCKS PER WEEK AVOIDS A THRASH CRASH

While each of the blocks that go into the weekly perspective are important and need to be accounted for, we're focusing mostly on your focus blocks in this book because they're the fuel for your best work and the anchors in your schedule. Once you start building your weekly schedule around your focus blocks and assert the boundaries, courage, and discipline to honor them, you'll have an easier time seeing where you can (and can't) put the two-hour chunks of your projects.

In addition, attending to focus blocks helps you see more clearly what's going on with your projects, as every project you do pulls against a limited reserve of focus blocks. Just because you coax your schedule to minimize the Swiss-cheese holes doesn't mean you're going to be able to put your best-work project in those slots—you likely have other projects you're behind on that will claim those newly found openings. So before we jump into roadmapping, it's worth assessing your current projects after you've carved out those focus blocks. As a general guideline, you want to make sure you have three free focus blocks that you can allocate to your best-work project, as that's enough to get and maintain momentum without having to cold-start the project every time you touch it.

If you can't find or create three focus blocks per week to work on your best-work project—even after you've dropped some projects and renegotiated other project timelines—consider whether it's worth putting it on hold while you finish up another project that's claiming your focus blocks. It may be better to hold off for a month and knock out a project or two, so you can build some consistent momentum with your best-work project rather than risking the demotivation of fits and starts on it. This is a dangerous proposition, I realize, as it can so easily be a way to avoid doing the work that scares you. But seeing steady progress is motivating enough for it to be worth the gamble. The trick is to avoid filling up the newly found focus blocks with yet another distracting project. Rather than commit to something new, use the *snowball method* if you have multiple projects that are eating the focus blocks you want to spend elsewhere.

As you use the Five Projects Rule and weekly blocks, you'll be able to create ever more space if you use the snowball method. The snowball method is a process of finishing a project to free up blocks you then apply on the next project. So if you have three projects each requiring a focus block a week to maintain, finish the project that you can get done the fastest, then apply its focus block on the next fastest-to-finish project. The second project will then be getting two focus blocks per week, which means you'll finish it at least twice as quickly once you finish the first project. It's "at least twice" because the slower a project moves now, the slower it tends to move in the future. When you're done with the second project, apply its two focus blocks to the third project, with the same effect. When you're done with this snowballing, you'll have three focus blocks to apply to your chosen project.

The "three focus blocks per week" guideline becomes especially important during the void stage of the project where you'll be thrashing and frustrated. With fewer blocks than that, you'll be more easily demotivated about the very conscious lack of real progress for the amount of effort you're putting into making the project go. Having a bad week with your project is tolerable; having what seems to be a bad month with your project can lead to a thrash crash that kills the project and your willingness to properly revive or eject it.

If you still can't free up three focus blocks to work on your best-work project, all is not lost. To riff on the Mexican proverb "an ant on the move does more than a dozing ox," an inchworm who stays on the path makes more progress than a hummingbird who flits from flower to flower. You'll likely have more head trash to contend with as you compare your rate of progress to others who have more focus blocks to spend on their projects, and you'll likely feel as if everything you do takes forever to finish. From one perspective, it *will* take you much longer to finish your project, but it's not because you're uniquely defective or doing something wrong—you just have other priorities and constraints to attend to. Stick with it and leave yourself lots of crumb trails (more on this later) to help you make the most use of your time.

IT'S TIME TO MAKE TIME

When they first hear about the Five Projects Rule and weekly block planning, many people's first response is "That's great, but I don't have time to figure all of that out." But by now you know you're not going to *find* the time somewhere for your best work; you have to make the time for your best work.

When you use the Five Projects Rule and weekly block planning, you end up with defaults and constraints that aid your planning and prioritization. Rather than recreating the wheel for every project, every day, and every week, you can use a process that's more like the shape sorters you likely started using in preschool or kindergarten. You have a small number of shapes (the Five Projects Rule) and each has parts that fit into a few slots in your week (block planning). Don't let the simplicity of the framework belie its power, and, remember, simple doesn't equal easy. But it's better to be simple and hard than complex and hard.

Two pieces of paper and a pencil are all you need to figure out what your five projects (for this quarter, month, and week) are and how to build your weekly block schedule, but I have some planners and aids ready-made for you on our book resources page.[1] There's no need for you to re-create something that millions of people have already used.

If you do nothing else, though, decide what your five projects are for the next quarter, month, and week. In the next chapter you'll learn how to roadmap a project and that project could either be your best-work project (if you have an open slot) or a project that needs to be completed to make space for your best-work project. Either way, you win.

1. You can find these planners at startfinishingbook.com/resources.

CHAPTER 5 TAKEAWAYS

▷ To start doing your best work, create space for a specific project and build from there.

▷ Chunking, linking, and sequencing are the key skills that will help you create space and build plans that work. The project pyramid shows how bigger projects contain smaller projects and how those smaller projects build momentum.

▷ The thirty-four common project words clearly show how projects are chunked, linked, and sequenced.

▷ The Five Project Rule is shorthand for "no more than five active projects per timescale" and helps prioritize and plan projects.

▷ Use the following kinds of blocks for block planning: focus blocks, social blocks, admin blocks, and recovery blocks.

▷ Three focus blocks per week per best-work project helps you maintain momentum, efficiency, and focus.

Nothing is particularly hard
if you divide it into small jobs.
HENRY FORD

BUILD YOUR PROJECT ROAD MAP

Now that you've made space for your project by using the
Five Projects Rule and creating a weekly block schedule, it's
time to break your project down into the chunks that you'll
get done during those blocks. The project pyramid will be in
play here too, but we'll also be looking at the ingredients that
make up your project.

The goal here is to build a project road map, which is a
specific kind of project plan that chunks, links, and sequences
the project over time. The road map helps us convert the
vertical list of to-dos into a horizontal, time-based plan. With
the vertical list, you have to do the sequencing work every
time you look at it. Thinking about time is hard enough to
start with, but when you add multiple chunks of multiple
projects to the picture, you jump from arithmetic to calculus
in terms of complexity and difficulty.

Your project road map will show you which chunks of
your best-work project you can put on deck *today* or *this week*,
rather than leaving your work stuck in Someday/Maybe Land.
But speaking of difficulty, let's start with how to make sure
you're not making the project harder than it needs to be from
the start.

OPEN FLOW WITH YOUR PROJECT BY BUILDING FROM YOUR GATES

A few years ago I got an email from a reader—let's call him Arnie—seeking advice on how to grow his (written) blog. In his email he mentioned that he wasn't good at writing and didn't enjoy it. A sentence or two later, he mentioned how much he loved talking and creating videos.

Being distant enough from his own stories, it was clear to me—and probably to you—that he was asking the wrong question and fundamentally pursuing his goals in the wrong way. He didn't need to grow his written blog; he needed to start a podcast or video blog.

What was so striking to me from his email was that the answer was right in front of him, but he just couldn't see it. While this may be an extreme anecdote, it's far from an isolated incident of the common counterproductive pattern of choosing harder-than-necessary ways to accomplish goals. If you're being honest with yourself, I bet you can come up with something you've done over the last couple of weeks that could have been done a lot easier if you had based it upon your advantages.

Rather than start your project on hard mode, why not take the upper hand by playing to your strengths? Playing to your strengths makes the project easier to do, and you'll find flow more often when you're using your strengths. The days of thriving creative giants are different precisely because they're in flow while doing their best work.

Strengths come in different varieties, though, and the acronym GATES is a handy way to consider what you should base your projects on. GATES stands for:

- ▶ **Genius.** What seems to be an expression of an inner creative force.
- ▶ **Affinities.** What you're drawn to do.
- ▶ **Talents.** What seems to be your native skills or capabilities.
- ▶ **Expertise.** What you've learned through experience and practice.
- ▶ **Strengths.** What seems to come easy for you.

For our present discussion, it's not important to dive into how we acquire and hone each element of our GATES, since positive feedback and continuous practice cultivates all of them. Once you have your GATES in play, you can start to build out how to overcome your tendency to make projects harder than they need to be. Stop for a moment and list some of your GATES; don't stop until you have about fifteen. I'll wait.

If you struggled to come up with fifteen, it's probably because you followed the common pattern of only putting recognized professional skills on the list, but those are just a small subset of GATES. Consider the following as GATES:

- ▶ Curating music, paintings, or art
- ▶ Decorating
- ▶ Organizing data in spreadsheets
- ▶ Interacting with kids or pets
- ▶ Knowing Greek mythology
- ▶ Woodworking
- ▶ Making cobblers
- ▶ Coming up with catchy names
- ▶ Performing improv
- ▶ Orienteering
- ▶ Throwing parties
- ▶ Building workflows
- ▶ Deep reading

I could go on, but you get the gist. Your list of GATES is unique to you, and while it's true that not all of them are relevant for your project, asking "Which of my GATES can I leverage to complete this project?" is a great place to start.

Consider the graph below that has a column for GATES, methods, and goals. *Methods* is the only new category here, and I mean for it to be broad enough to cover actions, strategies, tactics, or techniques, since they all relate to how you'll go about achieving a particular goal.

GATES	METHODS	GOALS

Most people find it easiest to work backward from the goal, but we're not going to move right into listing methods, since doing so divorces the methods from your GATES. Rather, we start with GATES on the left side, *then* fill out the methods in between.

Let's return to Arnie. Let's assume his goals were to build an audience and increase his business revenue. That would go in the right-hand column. What Arnie did, though, was put "writing" in his method column. He mistook the method for the goal.

But consider what it would look like if he *started* with his GATES and then filled in the method. In the left-hand column, he would put "talking" and "creating videos." It would then be clear that the pathway between his GATES and his goals would be podcasting and video blogging, and *only* doing as much writing as he absolutely had to do.

Your GATES may be more than just a sign of how to get a project done—they may be pointing to a deeper "purpose imprint" or identity. We're all born with a certain imprint for work that makes us come alive. Work that lets us wake up in the morning and know, deep down, we're doing what we're here to do. Work that sets us ablaze with purpose and, fully expressed in a healthy way, becomes a mainline to meaning, purpose, expression, and flow.

I call this imprint or identity your Sparketype. It's not about specific jobs, titles, industries, or fields. Yes, we often have fleeting glimpses of jobs, projects, teams, businesses, industries, causes, activities, adventures, endeavors, or moments that give us passing hits of "Yes, please, I'll take some of that!" But we don't know *why* we feel that way, we don't understand what made it so powerful for us, and it never lasts for long.

Truth is, your Sparketype operates more on the level of "source code." Think of it as the DNA-level driver for what makes you come alive. Discovering this unique imprint helps answer the question "What am I here to do?"

In my research I've identified ten Sparketypes: Maker, Maven, Scientist, Essentialist, Sage, Performer, Warrior, Advisor, Advocate, and Nurturer. How do you discover them? Interestingly, your GATES can serve as potential discovery signposts, since they often serve as pathways of expression for your Sparketype.

The more you integrate your GATES and Sparketype into the work you do in the world, the more your life and work will be deeply nourishing, on purpose, fully expressed, and in flow.

Jonathan Fields is the bestselling author of three books—his latest being *How to Live a Good Life: Soulful Stories, Surprising Science, and Practical Wisdom*—the executive producer of the popular *Good Life Project* podcast, and the creator of the Sparketype assessment. Go to Sparketype.com if you want to take the free assessment and see what Sparketype your GATES are pointing to.

It's true that Arnie may have eventually brute-forced his way to success, but damn if that wouldn't be the hard way. Think about how much discipline and courage he'd have to muster to continue to improve his writing, as well as how much head trash he'd have to work through to get there. A fraction of that energy spent using what he was already good at would have gone much, much further.

You may have noticed that Arnie discounted his GATES. That's also a common pattern. This is where your success pack comes in, as they can and will often reflect your GATES back to you. And if you seed it, they may also help you see how to weave your GATES into the methods to use to reach your goals.

While we've discussed the GATES framework in the context of a project, consistent use of your GATES across your life and work helps overcome head trash and having too few resources from the air sandwich. If you're playing from your weaknesses, it's much easier for shame and struggle stories to win out, and whatever resources you have don't go nearly as far. It's easier to identify your GATES when you apply them to a specific project.

BUILD A BUDGET FOR YOUR PROJECT

While a few projects can be completed with just your time, energy, and attention, most require some money to get done too. And even when money isn't *required* to get a project done, it usually makes it easier or quicker to do.

Few of us have money lying around to fuel discretionary projects. Even when we do have saving and investment habits, that money is either tied up or working for us in different ways. I've lived through many periods where there wasn't enough for the necessities, let alone the discretionary projects. I get it.

But there are always ways to reprioritize how to use what we have, and many of us are spending money to fill the empty spaces where meaning and fulfillment should be. We often buy cars, trips, meals, alcohol, entertainment, and status we don't need as a way to avoid the boredom, frustration, and alienation we feel in our lives and work. It's a cruel paradox:

the less we have, the more likely we are to compensate by spending money we don't have enough of to acquire things we don't need; but the more money we have, the more likely we are to continue to increase our expenses and still feel like we don't have enough.

Given that intelligent, creative people are prone to end up with acute and chronic creative constipation when they're not doing work that matters to them, it's even more important that they divert their money to fuel that work. Remember, creative people will either be actively creating something or actively destroying something, and the object of their destruction is the easiest target—themselves.

Also consider that budgeting for your project creates a positive boundary for your work rather than a negative (restrictive) boundary for it. The difference between being able to spend a certain amount for your project and not being able to spend more than that amount is subtle, but it's important. When we think about it positively, the goal isn't to focus on saving as much money as possible but rather to find the best ways to use the space we've created to get the project done. I've been talking about budgets as a way to fuel the project for exactly that reason.

Making budgets is like making plans in that it's an awareness-generating process, especially when you walk through the checklist of costs that just about any project may have. You may decide not to fund an item or be unable to, but considering it allows you to figure out how you're going to work around that item or to spot opportunities to create, find, or reprioritize spending to fund that item. Knowing that childcare would help you move your project along makes it easier to skip the dessert at dinner or leave the cute shirt on the rack and instead apply that money to your project fund.

Before we run through the checklist, start by considering what you would spend to complete your project. To give it some grip and reality, it's often simplest to consider your project budget as a fraction or multiple of your discretionary spending last month. For example, if you spent $500 last month between eating out and (discretionary) shopping, make your budget a fraction or multiple of that. The bigger the project, the more likely it needs to be a multiple, but it works out because you may be able to reallocate what you spend on those items *per month* to your project *per month* as you work the project through. If this is a project that you want your employer to fund, use a fraction or multiple of your monthly salary instead, since your case will probably need to be how much time it will save you (which decreases their expense in paying you) or how much the project will benefit the company (since that's what they pay you to do).[1]

We start with this step because it gives us a baseline to work from, otherwise we may overscrutinize every item on the checklist. From here, we'll work through the checklist and then adjust our budget from there.

---

1. How to make a budget for a company-funded project is considerably more complex than for a personally funded project. A common problem in business budgets is that they're centered only on expense factors rather than revenue factors, even though businesses can create revenue a lot easier than individuals can. As a shortcut, ask whoever makes your company budgets to explain how budgets are made and follow their guidance.

Here are the common items that may be a part of every project:

▸ **Professional support.** Editors, copywriters, media engineers, administrative assistants, photographers, lawyers, or consultants are common kinds of professional support that can make a big difference in the quality of the end product or the process of completing it. Whether you're paying someone to add competencies you don't have, paying to not have as many surprises that can be avoided, or simply paying to have someone do something you could do but don't need to do, you're shaving off time to complete the project or to make the results better.

▸ **Tools and apps.** You may be able to borrow someone else's tools and/or use some open-source stuff, but you may be better off just buying or renting the tools and apps you need to get the job done. Better to spend fifty dollars and have what you need than to spend hours every month getting and returning borrowed tools and hacking freeware.

▸ **Caretakers and personal support.** Childcare, elder care, and pet sitters can ensure your loved ones are safe, comfy, and not lonely while you're working on your project, but you may also consider yard care, housecleaning, and grocery delivery as well. It's also far cheaper to hire caretakers and personal

support than it is professional support; twenty-five dollars may only get you an hour of professional support but buy a half day or more of caretaking and personal support. People often underestimate how much their interruptions and distractions are weighing on them until they experience not being interrupted and distracted.

▸ **Lodging, offices, and table rent (coffee and tea).** I'm lumping these together because you may need different environments to get your work done, especially during the challenging parts of your work. There's a reason people hole themselves in cabins, hotels, and B&Bs to get their projects done. But paying for coffee and tea is often paying for a conducive work environment just as much as paying for an office or hotel is. Starbucks is right that it's not about the coffee; it's about paying to work in a place that helps you get your work done.

▸ **Food.** A lot of time and energy is spent in preparing and cleaning up meals, and you may find that it's worth it to you to eat out or have your food delivered. Or maybe it's that you love breakfast but hate making it, so between not making it and not eating or paying six dollars to start the day off well, the latter clearly makes more sense.

Once you've aggregated all the expenses mentioned, compare that to the baseline you started with. Professional support is what often breaks the budget, but you'll need to weigh that cost against the real costs of not having the support. And you may need to consider whether you need to have another project in front of this one to create the funds to fuel this project.

Sharing your budget with partners and family members often sparks great conversations about who can help. For instance, your partner may rather cover caretaking for you than pay someone else, but they may also rather pay for caretaking so they can do *their* best-work projects too. Or your friend who's an editor may exchange their expertise if you'll dog-sit for a week while they're on a trip.

Seeing what would fuel your project and how you're going to get it ahead of time helps avoid getting stuck or hemhawing about getting what you need when it's clear you need it. But you have to start with acknowledging that you and your work are worth it. If nothing else, remember what it's costing you *not to do* your best work.

DEADLINES GUIDE YOUR PROJECT; CAPACITY DRIVES YOUR PROJECT

Imagine that during a normal week, you set goals and deadlines that assume you'll be able to get ten units of work done. But, during a normal week, you actually get four units of work done.

Imagine that during light weeks, you set goals and deadlines that you'll be able to do six units of creative work. But, during those light weeks, you actually get four units of creative work done.

In this scenario, it's easy to see that the goals and deadlines aren't doing anything besides stressing you out. Set all the

JACQUETTE M. TIMMONS   YOUR MONEY NEEDS YOU TO GIVE IT DIRECTION

If you have a reactive relationship with money, you probably tend to fund your projects reactively too. This correlation isn't accidental.

Most of us have been conditioned to manage money by default, meaning you decide how to save, invest, and spend it based upon what you earn. An alternative way to manage your money is by design, meaning you first decide how much you want to save, invest, and spend and then ask, "How much do I need to earn to do these various things with my money?"

Shifting your mindset about money from "using what's left over" (by default) to "determining what I need" (by design) will profoundly affect your approach to money. It will also help with creating budgets for your projects because you'll develop the habit of factoring in the role of money at the outset (proactive) rather than as an afterthought (reactive).

For money to fulfill its job in your life, it needs you to give it direction—even when money is tight. Creating a budget for your projects is a form of telling money what it is you want it to do for you regarding your project.

And don't let the desire to get the numbers "just right" stump you. As you make progress on your project, you'll get feedback that will help you adjust your budget accordingly—money will always give you feedback about the quality of your choices and highlight for you when you're being proactive . . . or not.

Jacquette M. Timmons works as a financial behaviorist and focuses on the human side of money. She's the author of *Financial Intimacy: How to Create a Healthy Relationship with Your Money and Your Mate* and creator of The Comfort Circle dinner series.

deadlines and goals you want, but it's the four units of creative work that matters.

Those four units of creative work are your true capacity. When it comes to moving your projects forward, it's the only thing that really matters. Goals and deadlines are just tools you use to create commitments and expectations you can't possibly meet.

Unfortunately you may have a pattern of using a backward-planning process that starts with the deadline and then walks backward to the milestones and targets you need to hit to make that deadline.

The backward-planning process is a great method for projects with hard deadlines and for helping you see major elements of the project, but it doesn't work as well for our purposes for two major reasons:

▷ It's easy to build a plan that doesn't fit reality because we often fail to consider the *other* projects we have going at the time with their own deadlines; so more often than not, the plan is doomed before you finish making it.

▷ The projects that matter most very often don't have hard deadlines to them. They're usually not urgent, there's little social pressure to do them, and their outcomes are generally more amorphous than others. To address the lack of hard deadlines, many people try to create aspirational deadlines for themselves, but far too often those aspirational deadlines are "good to do by" dates.

When we build from our capacity rather than the deadline, we get closer to carrying the amount of projects we can actually finish. Doing so means less planning and adjusting plans, fewer project collisions, and less frustration about the things we didn't get to this week. And while it feels like we're giving up something by focusing on fewer projects, the whole idea of the red line is that it's what we're actually able to do anyway.

The added benefit of basing your plans on your capacity is that it helps to shift your focus from results to process. If what's driving those units of work is creating and firewalling your focus blocks, then you can rework your schedule such that you get more focus blocks. If the results happen from a shift in environment or tools, then you can explore that more. Or maybe it's the kinds of projects or how you're using your GATES at play.

But let's not throw backward planning out with the bathwater. It can be incredibly useful as a tool to limit the scope of your project or to triage your projects.

The backward-planning process is useful for:

▶ Constraining the size of the project because you only have so many focus blocks, and it probably alters how much you're able to work on other projects.

▶ Illuminating milestones and deadlines that you might otherwise miss while roadmapping.

▶ Hitting project deadlines that are inherently anchored to dates, such as taxes, holidays, recurring deadlines.

So if backward planning works well for you, use it, but then adjust your deadlines based on what you can actually do, which may mean that you need to drop other projects to free up the focus blocks to get it done in the timeline available. Intentionally and proactively dropping projects so you can finish a project that matters is much better than *not* doing that and continuing to carry too many projects.

DON'T FORGET TO ACCOUNT FOR RELAY TIME

Another consideration to think about before you build out your road map is the relay time you'll need for projects that involve other people. Relay time is the waiting time that happens every time a project changes hands. We sometimes forget to include relay time in our planning because it's not active time.

Why *relay time*? Projects can be like relay races where each person is running as fast as they can to hand off the baton to someone else. But the reality is that all it takes is one bad handoff or one person to sandbag the relay for the *whole thing* to slow down.

For example, let's say you send your work to a coworker to review at the end of the day. Depending on what they have going on, it's unlikely that they'll be able to take a look at it until midmorning the next day. But if they're in meetings or working against a tight deadline, it could be days or weeks until they're able to flip it back to you. If you have a sequential project—one that requires step A to be completed before you move on to step B—or the person's perspective is required before you work on any other part of the project, the time is clicking but your project isn't going anywhere.

I mentioned above that two conditions create additional relay time: (1) bad handoffs, and (2) someone slowing down the race (typically because they're overloaded and are unintentionally bottlenecking the race).

Bad handoffs occur for three reasons:

▸ You're unclear about what you need.

▸ You're communicating in channels or ways where the baton isn't being received.

▸ You're not indicating that it *is* a relay task and who's running next.

For instance, take the far-too-common process of sending an email to multiple collaborators with "Thoughts?" or "What do you think?" as a request. In this case, all three reasons are at play. "Thoughts?" is too broad a question, as it's not clear what the tension points are most of the time, so collaborators have to work especially hard to respond. The usual result is that your request goes into the "stuff to think about" bucket that's already overfull. If it's via email, it's not in a channel that's conducive for actual conversation, so it's a bad handoff there. And since it's sent to multiple collaborators, it's not clear that it's a relay task and who's running next. (If I could, I would ban "Thoughts?" and "What do you think?" from *all* team communication, as there are *always* better questions to ask to move the ball forward and foster collaboration.)

Addressing bad handoffs often helps with someone slowing down the relay since it lowers the amount of work that the next person has to do. But there are also collaborators who slow down the relay because of their schedule, capacity, and preferences. In each case, you need to consider when and how to hand off the baton to each person. For example, if you're working with a collaborator in an earlier time zone than you, and you need something from them today, you'll need to send the work to them earlier or wait until the next day. If your boss is prone to ask twenty questions or the same kinds of questions every time you run something by them, then not answering those questions before you hand them the baton is going to slow down the relay. They *will* ask those questions—you may as well preempt them so they can address what you need.

Rather than addressing all the strategies for mitigating relay time in this book, my main goal here is to put relay time into the mix for consideration as you build your road map. The "Upgrade Your Clumps" section on page 144 provides a quick way to address relay time, but if you know your projects are being unreasonably delayed due to relay time, then you may want to focus more on smoother, more strategic handoffs with your collaborators.

HOW TO BUILD YOUR PROJECT ROAD MAP

With the ingredients of your project discussed thus far, we can start to build a project road map. Before we start building the road map for your project, these four rules will serve you well:

▸ **If you're going to be (hand)writing, write in pencil or something erasable.**

▸ **Make multiple passes.**

▸ **Have enough space to have a messy area and a clean area.** *Space* could mean multiple sheets of paper or different portions of a whiteboard; in a digital context, it could be different sections of a document, with one area being the "scratch" area.

▸ **Embrace your top-down or bottom-up planning styles.** Some people are skilled at chunking projects from bigger chunks to smaller ones, but they get overwhelmed with all the smaller chunks. Others find that building from smaller chunks makes more sense to them, but they have trouble with how big the top-level projects feel once they've put them together. No one style is better than the other; the Five Projects Rule, weekly block schedule, and the roadmapping process you'll be working through address these challenges.

You are encouraged to make the mistakes of making chunk sizes too big, forgetting some chunks, not seeing how they link together, and putting them in the wrong sequence. Think of this exercise more like putting building blocks together with pages missing from the instructions and some pieces you can't see because they're hidden behind others. If you're planning effectively, you'll be reworking your plan multiple times. (I know, it's a paradox.)

It's time to start playing with the conceptual toys we've been unpacking in this chapter.

1 START YOUR CHUNK LIST

Your chunk list is, unsurprisingly, a list of all the top-of-mind chunks of the project. During this phase, don't worry about the size of the chunks. It's not necessary to think about the fifteen-minute tasks of the project, but if they come to you, don't fight them. Use the universal action words on page 104.

The goal of this step isn't to get all the chunks of the project in the first go, but just to start with what's right in front of you.

You may find it easier to mindmap your project rather than just listing action items. Whichever technique you use, use one of your messy spaces for this part of the project. And leave room, as you'll be adding chunks in another pass.

2 SORT AND LINK YOUR CHUNKS

If your project starts with a big objective word such as *develop*, it contains chunks that would begin with words such as *research*, *plan*, *design*, and *create*, and would probably be linked to other similar-sized project chunks that begin with words such as *publish* or *kick off*.

Knowing these patterns, you can sort and link your chunks into the right arrangements. People who are strong at spatial thinking often find it helpful to split out the chunks into a hierarchy from quarter-sized down to week-sized, since it makes the next step easier, but that also causes some people to spin out. If you're of the latter variety, don't worry about creating a hierarchy—you have other GATES you can use to help out here.

3 SEQUENCE YOUR CHUNKS

To start sequencing your chunks, you still don't need to do anything besides look at how the verbs in front of the chunks relate to each other. If the verb is *publish*, you can't do that without creating and editing something, but you usually can't create something without planning and researching it. Whether it's Research ▸ Plan ▸ Create ▸ Edit ▸ Publish, or Plan ▸ Research ▸ Create ▸ Edit ▸ Publish, as far a verb sequence goes, it's usually pretty clear. It can always be Research ▸ Plan ▸ Research ▸ Create ▸ Edit ▸ Publish, with the understanding that the first round of research is *survey* research and the second round is *deep* research. Survey research helps you figure out if the project is worthy and create the plan; deep research helps you do the work.

Once sequencing begins, it's pretty normal for people to realize they missed some chunks, so you may need to add some chunks to get a proper sequence. That's great; it's exactly why you're doing this now.

It's often helpful to do some slight renaming of the chunks, as I did above and in the last chapter, to give more specificity and meaning (remember the SMART acronym). So perhaps you need to switch *research* to *conduct initial research* or *survey* once you start sequencing chunks, to separate it from the other researching you'll do after you've committed to the project. At this stage, it can be helpful to keep the original verb so you remember its chunk size—for example, "Research (Survey)"—as it's far too easy to lose that context and forget how it's linked or contained in other chunks.

Because sequencing focuses on arranging chunks in the order that they need to be done, it's natural to start thinking about *when* those chunks need to happen. Sequencing isn't scheduling, though, and we're not quite to the scheduling stage. If it bugs you to not write down when something needs to happen, you can always write the deadline—for example, "Research (Survey) by March 31st" or "Develop TPS Report (March 31st)."

4 CLUMP YOUR CHUNKS

Clumping is the opposite of chunking in that it's the process of organizing smaller chunks by the larger chunks that contain them. To continue with our building blocks metaphor, clumping is putting pieces together into larger, linked units, like two separately built wheels and axles coming together to form the chassis of a building-block truck.

The project pyramid gives us a default way to clump our chunks, and the sequenced chunks from above clump into a bigger, coherent chunk. So the sequence above—Research ▸ Plan ▸ Create ▸ Edit—clumps together to a bigger Publish project. If we estimate that each of the chunks in the lower-level sequence will take a day, we see that the Publish project is a week-sized project; if we estimate each lower-level chunk will take a week, that particular Publish project is a month-sized project.

Clumping helps us build our road map by allowing us to switch to a higher-level time perspective so we can better shape that perspective. Most projects that matter will span over months and quarters, and we need to be able to shape our time at those levels, but we don't need to see the lower-level chunks at those higher levels. If we clump our project into, say, four month-sized chunks and we plan on doing one of those month-sized chunks each for the next four months, then when we're doing our monthly goal setting and planning for next month, we don't need to think about the parts of the project that follow next month. We can think about them when we've finished next month's projects and the next leg of the project is upon us.

5 UPGRADE YOUR CLUMPS

After you've created your larger clumps, it's time to check if you need to *upgrade* some of these clumps into the next larger size in the time perspective. By *check* I mean you almost always will need to do some upgrading based on the triggers below.

There are five triggers that suggest you should upgrade the clump in question to the next higher chunk size:

▸ You have no idea how long it will take to do the clump.

▸ You're not competent at the work involved to complete the clump.

▸ The clump depends on someone else completing a chunk of work of that chunk's size—that is, if you're looking at a clump of week-sized chunks and someone else needs to do one of those chunks, then you need to upgrade the clump.

▸ The clump contains more than five chunks.

▸ One of the chunks in the clump will take more of that chunk size of time to complete. For example, if the clump contains month-sized projects, it would normally be a quarter-sized clump, but if one of those month-level chunks will actually take multiple months to complete, upgrade it to a year-sized clump.

If all five conditions are present, you don't need to upgrade something five times so that it can't get done. It's often better to add an additional unit of time to the project, though. For instance, if you end up with a month-sized clump after upgrading once, and you see that another trigger is in play, add another month to the project's timeline. If another is in play, add another month, which is essentially an upgrade to the next higher chunk size anyway.

These planning factors account for the displacement, stalls, wait times, project cascades, competing priorities, thrashing, unforeseeable life challenges, and overestimation that will happen with projects that matter. While they don't *explain* why projects can take so long to finish, they at least give some guide rails that help us create more realistic road maps.

To continue with our example clump—Research ▸ Plan ▸ Create ▸ Edit—that we've already decided would be a month-sized project, if the Create chunk seems as if it will take three weeks to do, upgrading it to a quarter-sized project would be prudent. Remember, it's not that a quarter-sized project will take the full quarter but that it will require prioritization at that time perspective and below. Seeing that it needs to sit at that level ensures that you don't stack too many quarter-sized projects that you won't be able to finish.

As you get better at practicing the five keys and getting projects done, you may decide that you don't need to upgrade projects per the suggestions above, or you might decide to alter the way you upgrade them. For instance, you may decide that it's better to double the time you think something will take rather than shift it to the next higher time perspective. But if you're chronically overcommitted and not finishing what you start, try using the guidelines to see if it helps. Yes, you'll commit to fewer projects, but you'll also finish more of what matters and carry fewer stalled and dead projects too.

6 OVERLAY YOUR CHUNKS ON A TIMELINE

The last step of upgrading is to check that the sequence of the chunks still appears coherent and logical. Like above, you may need to do some slight renaming of the chunks to do so, but at this stage of the process, there's less of a concern about forgetting chunk size since you'll be renaming, linking, and sequencing at a fixed time perspective.

The roadmapping method builds the timeline from how long we guesstimate the chunks of the project will take to get done. Upgrading and resequencing mean that we can simply lay the project out.

To start overlaying your chunks on a timeline, you have to start with a time perspective that corresponds to the perspective of your project. It sounds obvious, but laying out a month-sized project on a year-sized timeline isn't helpful because you wouldn't be able to see the week-sized chunks and daily blocks that you'd need for that level of detail and context. At the year-sized timeline, the *lowest* you would generally want to go is two sizes under it, so you might be able to meaningfully put month-sized projects on that timeline.

This rule holds for all time perspectives; for example, if you're looking at a month-sized timeline—a.k.a. a calendar—getting into the nitty-gritty of what's happening in the hours and minutes of your days wouldn't be meaningful. At most, you would want to put fixed events and appointments on the day, which is what you're probably already doing.

As a general guideline, use a timeline that's one size larger than your largest chunk so you can see how that chunk relates to other projects. The exception here is year-sized projects, unless you're comfortable looking at a three-year perspective. Three-year timelines are outside of most people's mental headlights and planning confidence and thus can cause more anxiety than clarity. People usually have an intuitive sense of the next year-sized project that their current year-sized project rolls into or sets up.

The inverse is also useful: if you want to build a timeline that charts your focus blocks, you should use no larger than a monthly timeline. The additional advantage of using this rule is that it will help prevent the overoptimistic thinking that you can lay out exactly how you'll use your focus blocks five weeks from now. If you want to have a sense of where your focus blocks will get you five weeks from now, you must think up two time perspectives, to the monthly level. (I told you it was easy to slip between time perspectives.)

Let's assume that the Create chunk of the quarterly Publish project we've been coaxing got upgraded to a month-sized project because of the size of the work being created. When we did our clumping, let's say we added a Staging chunk because we anticipated needing to do a few things to make the edited work ready for show. Our road map might thus look like the figure below.

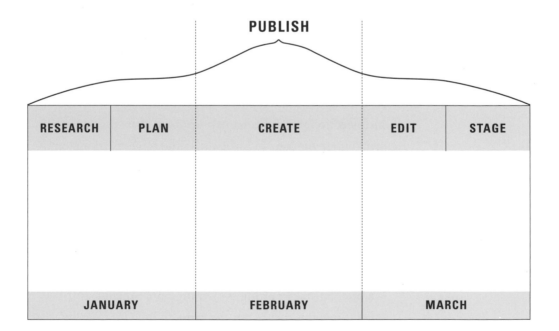

You can see why you wouldn't want to include the focus-block level—the road map would be so busy that it would cease to be useful. Additionally, we don't *need* to go to that level at this stage since, when we're close to doing the next chunk of the project, we can pick the timeline horizon that's appropriate for the work.

Roadmapping this way makes it easier to adjust the larger chunks—or the whole thing—if you need to. For instance, let's say that in the project above, something happens at the end of January that displaces your ability to do the Create leg of the project. Rather than changing the dates of a lot of tasks or blocks, you can simply move the Create leg of the project (and the parts of the project that follow) into whatever month makes sense. Do yourself a favor and add a Review chunk to the front of the Create leg, so you realistically plan for a crawl rather than a gallop as you get back into the project.

When you build road maps this way, you can transpose other projects to the same timeline to see how things are stacking up, since you've fixed the timeline horizon and time perspective. That said, having a handful of projects roadmapped this way is a bit much (unless you like playing Tetris), but that's the beauty of the project pyramid: you don't have to know in advance what all the moving pieces are. You just need to know how many projects of that size might be stacking up on you, and when it's time to get working on those projects, you can "activate" the chunks that are relevant in that time perspective or do some roadmapping on the fly to see how you're going to get the work done in that period.

7 SCHEDULE YOUR CHUNKS

We often mistake putting something on a timeline as scheduling, but they're not the same thing. Committing to do something "next week"—that is, putting it on a timeline—is weak sauce; committing to do it Wednesday morning at 10:00 or, even better, during Wednesday's focus block, pushes it one step closer to done.

How you schedule is obviously going to depend on what tools you use, but it also depends on what size project you're talking about. Scheduling a month-sized project means that you first check your schedule and other commitments to ensure that you have enough room for it that month, *then* you schedule its week-sized chunks and blocks to get it done. If you're using a digital or standard calendar, it may be harder to figure out where to show that you've committed to a month-sized project. Blocks are easier to schedule, though, since most digital and many print calendars are built around the idea of setting appointments, so you can convert their appointment features for blocks.

Many people get tripped up, though, because they try to schedule chunks too far in advance and then get frustrated when reality doesn't look like their plans. Again, we return to the project pyramid. If you're doing your monthly planning, you should only be scheduling and prioritizing at that perspective, which means looking at the quarter for context and scheduling week-sized chunks. If you're doing your weekly planning, it's the same thing: look at the month for context, schedule blocks for the week.

Keep in mind that the further out you schedule creative projects, the more likely it is that you'll need to adjust that schedule. On the flip side, the less advance planning you do, the less likely you are to complete the project in the first place. It's a balancing act, but remember that the point of a plan isn't to straitjacket you but rather to help you drive your project to done.

If you've been reading along without doing the steps I've listed above, I encourage you to grab some paper and actually apply the steps to a focus block or two. If it made sense when you read it, that's great; you can immediately apply it to your best-work project. If it didn't make sense, that's also great; you can pick it up by applying it. To keep with the math analogy with which I started the chapter, doing this is much like doing multiplication tables; with repetition, you'll see the patterns, but you may not see the patterns without the repetition.

Once you're done, celebrate! The work you've done is part of your best work and it's probably been challenging. But you've made it clear what your next steps are with your project, which means you're one step closer to being proud of the best work you've released into the world.

CHAPTER 6 TAKEAWAYS

▷ A project road map is a project plan that places chunks of a project on a timeline.

▷ Build projects from your GATES— genius, affinities, talents, expertise, and strengths—from the beginning to make it easier to get the project done.

▷ Creating a budget for your project helps avoid snags and stall-outs, and even when a project doesn't require money, funding a project can make it better.

▷ Use deadlines to guide your project, but remember that it's your capacity that drives your project no matter what the deadline is.

▷ When you're working with collaborators— and almost all best work projects have collaborators—make sure to build relay time into your road map.

▷ As you work through building your road map, write in pencil and embrace the mistakes you're going to make.

I'm not afraid of storms,
for I'm learning to sail my ship.
LOUISA MAY ALCOTT, *Little Women*

KEEP FLYING BY ACCOUNTING FOR DRAG POINTS

Engineers have to deal with a fascinating tension: the faster the vehicle they're designing is meant to go, the more they'll have to account for the different ways drag is going to affect it. In a way, drag is reality pushing against their designs.

In a similar vein, reality will push against the design of your project road map. Rather than gravity and wind resistance being the dominant forces creating drag, people tend to be the dominant sources of drag for your project.

The person who's most likely to push against the momentum of your project, though, is you, so let's start there.

YOUR NO-WIN SCENARIOS ARE KEEPING YOU FROM THRIVING

The more you do your best work and start thriving, the more you may start pumping the brakes. Many of us ingrain in ourselves a story that to be successful in our work or lives, we have to give up something important to us.

While the details of the no-win scenarios we create for ourselves vary, they tend to look like one of the three general stories that follow:

If you don't address the no-win scenarios you're telling yourself, they're going to be the unwelcome gift that keeps on giving because you'll always put a cap on the level of happiness, success, or flourishing that you'll allow yourself. Fortunately, once you see the no-win scenario you've created or accepted, it's simple to defang. (Remember: simple doesn't equal easy.)

THE SUCCESS WILL WRECK MY RELATIONSHIPS TALE

We all know someone who estranged themselves from their family, friends, and loved ones because of their (seemingly) single-minded pursuit of success. We've also experienced scenarios where somebody excelled and others were hurt, bitter, or envious about it, whether it was the smart sibling whose success was used as a yardstick for their other siblings, a friend who got the hot girl/guy that the others pined for, or the promotion that created a wedge in your work-buddy group. Because the fallout of these occurrences is so common and devastating, it's easy to encode a story that looks like "If I win, I hurt someone."

The difficulty with untangling this particular no-win scenario is that there are shared expectations that need to be addressed because relationships *are* shared expectations. One party may not want to let an expectation go or see that their expectation is preventing our self-actualization. Furthermore, we may be in relationships with people who consciously or unconsciously don't want us to grow and flourish because of their own insecurities, needs, and shortcomings. We don't get to define what type of spouse, friend, sibling, or aunt we want to be in a vacuum.

But we also can't blindly accept the definitions and expectations others have of us either, for it's all too common for people to expect or want us to be the supporting character in their story. To be clear, we're all supporting characters in each other's stories, but we're not *solely* supporting characters, and too many people don't allow themselves or get to be the stars in their own stories.

To untangle this no-win scenario, you're going to need to practice intention, boundaries, and courage. You're also going to have some hard conversations.

THE SUCCESS VERSUS VIRTUE MYTH

Another version of the no-win scenario is the Success Versus Virtue myth, and there's a host of variations on this one.

Here are a few different variations on this theme:

▶ **The Starving Artist myth.** This myth counterpoises creativity, authenticity, or craft with financial success. If your art starts selling well, it means you've sold out. So the story goes.

▶ **The Nice Guys Finish Last myth.** Yes, this is very similar to the previous kind of scenario, but it switches the focus from harming others to harming your own integrity or virtue. Better to be a person of character and not win than be a winner who sacrifices their own character.

▶ **The Rich People Are Bad People myth.** Rich people, the story goes, have cheated, stolen, oppressed, manipulated, or generally schmucked their way into wealth. That religious and spiritual traditions reinforce this only adds to the truthiness of the story.

In each case, some success state—wealth, achievement, fame, power, influence, etc.—is pitted against some virtue—honesty, generosity, authenticity, creativity, kindness, etc. To have the former, you have to compromise the latter. Or, even worse, if you work your way into having the former, you have to feel guilty or unsettled by it and work harder to make sure you're being a good person.

JEFF GOINS   THE MYTH OF THE STARVING ARTIST

The world usually doesn't look kindly on those with creative dreams. We give these creative souls all kinds of well-intentioned advice. "Be careful," we say, even if only in our minds. "Don't risk too much. Be sure you have a backup plan. Because you could starve."

What we often forget, though, is the starving artist story is a myth. And like all myths, it has the power to shape our lives—if we believe it. Those of us who believe the myth of the starving artist end up taking safer routes in life. We become lawyers instead of actors, bankers instead of poets, doctors instead of painters. We hedge our bets and hide from our true callings. Nobody wants to struggle, after all, so we keep our passions as hobbies and follow predictable paths toward mediocrity.

But there's another story worth considering. The story of the thriving artist. What if you could do your best creative work and you didn't have to starve to do it? What if you could thrive?

In the late Renaissance, artists were often well paid and as a result earned a place among society's elite. Today, we're experiencing a similar resurgence of talent—a New Renaissance of sorts—in which creatives of all types are waking up to their potential. They neither have to starve nor sell out. They can thrive. We all can. It just comes down to the story we believe.

Jeff Goins is a writer, speaker, and entrepreneur. He is the bestselling author of five books, including *The Art of Work: A Proven Path to Discovering What You Were Meant to Do* and *Real Artists Don't Starve: Timeless Strategies for Thriving in the New Creative Age.* His award-winning blog, *Goins, Writer,* is visited by millions of people every year.

It's true that we have plenty of examples of people who have managed to accrue success at the cost of their integrity. People will sell their soul or others' bodies for a buck. People will step on other people's necks to get four inches ahead. People will cut corners while still selling the square.

But there's no necessary connection between the two. There are plenty of examples of people who are successful *and* have integrity. There are also plenty of examples of unsuccessful people who lack character.

To extrapolate the journalist and biographer Robert Caro's point about power, success doesn't alter your character—it reveals your character. It can also test your character simply because the more successful you become, the more momentous and impactful your choices will become at the same time that more people will want your attention and resources.

To untie this particular no-win scenario, then, requires reframing the tension.

Here are three simple ways to do so:

▸ **Who is a model of someone who has managed to be successful and virtuous?** Your models will be different from mine, and they can be historical or present. If they were able to do it, why can't you?

▸ **Consider what virtue you think is in jeopardy.** What specific actions or behaviors would violate that virtue? Is it necessary to do those actions or behaviors in order for you to be successful?

▸ **How might winning or being successful allow you to be more virtuous?** Would you be better able to support or engage with what matters most to you?

You're too creative and resourceful to believe that you can't be successful and a good person. Yes, be on guard for missteps of character, but don't assume that you must take them to get ahead.

THE WHAT IF I CAN'T DO IT AGAIN? TRAP

The What If I Can't Do It Again? no-win scenario is a particularly insidious one for high achievers since we continually find ourselves doing well without much effort and preparation—so much so that we approach projects knowing that we can coast through them. At the same time, we know that there's a big difference between the results when we actually show up to win versus coasting, but this knowledge and practice ends up working against us. If we really stand tall and are seen for what we can do, we'll set a high standard that—gulp—we may not be able to do again.

So in order to prevent the second failure, we pick a success level and amount of effort that ensures that we can top ourselves in the future. The convenient upside to this is that we also don't have to choose what we'll be truly excellent in. We can continue to dabble, be better than the average bear, and collect our hodgepodge of third-place trophies with the smug, knowing grin of how much harder the people who won first and second place worked to get there.

The reason this no-win scenario is so hard to untie is because deep under the top-line question of "What if I can't do it again?" is a fear of losing the fun and freedom that comes with being a dabbler and polymath. Mastery and excellence require continual work, failure, and intention—we have to dig in to sweat the details and execution *after* it's fun, to get to the different kind of fun and freedom that comes with being an accomplished master of our craft.

Additionally, the What If I Can't Do It Again? trap overlooks that, along the way, we'll accrue more experience, people, and resources to do it better next time. Of course, we'll also escalate our goals and project scope, but that's what it means to be in that arena. At any given point in our lives, we're better than we were two months ago. Just as we should assume the sun will rise tomorrow because it rose today, we should also assume that we'll be two months better two months from now.

So perhaps it's true that this current version of yourself won't be able to do it again. Luckily for you, the better, stronger, and wiser version of yourself, playing your best game, will probably be able to do it. Success is cumulative; the shots you take today don't take from the shots you'll have in the future—they add to them.

Have the courage and faith that when the next dragon comes, you'll be able to slay it. Despite what it can sometimes seem, the fact that you've made it to here is evidence that you can make it to there.

And you *might* fail next time around, but better to try something with all your heart that might not work than to continue to go for the easy wins. Do you really need another third-place trophy?

TRANSCEND THE SAFE PLAY OF MEDIOCRITY

Let's take a look at the two prongs of no-win scenarios the way we've been talking about them. Avoiding failure needs no real explanation—no one wants to fail or be embarrassed or humiliated.

But when you have one of the beliefs above about success—that it will cause relational harm, that you'll have to be less virtuous, or that you'll eliminate your ability to be free or have fun—then those are some dragons you'll also want to avoid. The only way to avoid them is to be just successful enough to not risk them. If you stay far enough away from the dragons, they can't bite you.

The sad truth is that there's likely a small number of people in your life who will get mad, upset, or frustrated by your mediocrity, especially if your mediocrity is tied to your being attentive to their needs, priorities, or goals.

They will get mad, upset, or frustrated by your failures, and they *may* get mad, upset, or frustrated by your success.

Thus mediocrity is the safe play. No dragons can bite you, and you won't create more dragons when you overcome the one in front of you.

Mediocrity being the safe play is only partially true, though. It's true in the short term and in the day-to-day decisions and compromises you have to make: keep your head down, check the box, avoid the heat today.

But in the long run, it's the worst thing for your thriving in life and your career. Whose work do you remember that's a product of their keeping their head down, checking the box, and avoiding the heat? What important change in our culture has come from that? How many kids do you know who are thriving whose parents let them choose easy, safe options?

We're no more able to thrive by being mediocre than a fish is able to thrive in a shallow puddle. Sure, the fish may survive, but until they connect back with the deep waters and others of their school, they will always be a sunny day away from disaster.

We don't overcome no-win scenarios by choosing mediocrity; we overcome them by rejecting the stories that create them and doing our best work that creates success, happiness, and character.

SETH GODIN   ONLY THE TALL POPPY GETS THE FULL SUNLIGHT

Why choose mediocrity?

After all, it seems more fun to be extraordinary. To search for excellence. To be the one and only, the best in your field.

And yet there's a lot to be said for mediocre. Mediocre is another word for average. For fitting in. For doing precisely what's expected of you—pleasing as many people as possible.

Inherent in mediocrity is a degree of safety. The mediocre alternative is the standard one, and if you're the standard, it's easy to defend your actions. In every herd of antelope, there are a few outliers, dancing around the forward edges of the herd, teasing the lions. And there are a few at the rear, a little slow, the first to get picked off in the hunt. But the antelope in the middle of the pack is reassured to know that it's safe, isolated from the rest of the world.

We were taught this pack behavior in school. Middle school is a lot easier to survive if no one notices you, after all. And those lessons stick.

The problem? When our desire to matter collides with our need to feel safe. While being mediocre may *feel* safe, it no longer is. Because only the exceptional performers earn our attention, only the outliers have room to thrive and grow.

In many cultures there's the myth of the fate of the tall poppy. They say that it's the tall poppy that gets cut down, so you better not reach too far. The truth is, though, that it's only the tall poppy that gets the sunlight, and only the tall poppy that reaches its potential and is able to contribute what it's capable of.

Seth Godin is the author of nineteen international bestsellers, translated into thirty-six languages, that have changed the way people think about work, among them *Unleashing the Ideavirus*, *Permission Marketing, Purple Cow, Tribes, The Dip, Linchpin, Poke the Box*, and *All Marketers Are Liars*. He writes the most popular marketing blog in the world and speaks to audiences around the world. He is the founder of the altMBA, the founder and former CEO of Squidoo, the former vice president of direct marketing at Yahoo!, and the founder of the pioneering online startup Yoyodyne.

DON'T BE DOWN WITH OPP
(OTHER PEOPLE'S PRIORITIES)

If our project and priorities existed in a vacuum, they'd be far easier to get done. While we'd still thrash along the way and have to show up to do our work, we wouldn't have to manage our inner battles along with others'.

Alas, our priorities and projects exist alongside other people's priorities and other projects. Other people's priorities (hereafter OPP) seem similar to competing priorities, but the significant difference between OPP and competing priorities is that competing priorities are about our own accepted priorities rather than other people's priorities that we accommodate, acknowledge, or accept. If we accept OPP as our own, then they *do* become competing priorities, at least until we do some internal reflection and realize that there's value or intention misalignment.

For instance, many people follow pathways that make their parents and family happy. Whether it's assuming the family business or becoming the praiseworthy doctor or lawyer, many people grind through educational gauntlets, jump through political hoops, and fit themselves into clothes that never hang right because they're advancing someone else's priorities. Burnout, red convertibles, and broken hearts are predictable outcomes for pursuing OPP for too long.

Less extreme examples abound in our work and personal lives and at the project level. It could be that your boss's priorities shift and the project they once were behind gets kicked to the Island of Deprioritized Projects. Your partner's health and sanity may take a dive and your partner needs additional quality time with you. Your parents' downsizing project might become a storage problem for you as heaps of random stuff become yours to process.

Here are a few rules of OPP to consider:

- The longer your project takes you to complete, the more OPP you'll have to contend with.

- The more important your project is to you, the more OPP you'll have to contend with.

- There will never be a day in which OPP will go away. The world won't align so that everyone takes their priorities from your plate and makes your priorities their own. Consider how much OPP you end up managing on your birthday; if *any* day is going to be the day in which OPP subsides, it should be your birthday.

- If you aren't clear about your priorities with yourself and other people, you'll continually be beset by OPP.

- The more you bend and accommodate OPP, the more you'll have to bend and accommodate OPP.

The rules of OPP and boundaries are heavily interlinked. Maintaining strong boundaries helps sway the daily disruptions of OPP, since you have the right yeses and nos already set up to defer to. If it's well established that you spend Saturday doing planned adventures with your kids and family, then even if there's a really good reason for someone to ask you to do something on Saturday, it's a different conversation than if there's a history of co-opting you on Saturdays. Similarly, if you have a positive boundary such that you work on creative projects in the morning, people know that you can't be co-opted in the morning.

Here's how to address OPP as it comes up during your project:

▸ **For OPP that you accept or will accommodate, create the space and time in your schedule to do so.** This gives you a "yes and when" response that's less murky than "I'll get around to it." For example, if your dad calls you because he wants to talk, but it's actually not urgent, you can let him know you'll call him Wednesday night when you can give him your full attention. If you know that weekly is the right communication pulse with him, creating the positive boundary such that you talk with him every Wednesday may also prevent in-the-moment negotiations.

▸ **For OPP that you don't or can't accept, be clear that it's a no rather than a maybe.** It's better to establish this earlier rather than later. If it's a relationship that matters, you may need to find an acceptable alternative. That said, remember that "no" can be a complete sentence.

▸ **For OPP that you can't authentically accept and also can't outright reject or renegotiate, your best bet may be to go covert and advance your project in your own personal time.** For instance, your boss may not like the fact that you're working on a side hustle or nonprofit, but they can't say much if you're working on it during your lunch break or off-hours. If you go this route, it's important to avoid any discussion about your project with or in the presence of derailers (more on derailers to follow). If talking to your dad about how your book is coming along derails you, when he asks how your day or week has been, avoid mentioning anything about how your book is coming along, even if it's been a good week.

CAN YOU WEAVE OPP INTO YOUR PROJECT?

The above strategies assume that there's a conflict between OPP and your priorities and projects, but it's often the case that you can weave OPP into your project. The advantage of doing this is that you may be able to add some people to your success pack who may have otherwise been on the sidelines. In many cases, when people are kept on the sidelines of projects that matter to you, they tend to gravitate toward being derailers and naysayers; when they're on the sidelines, you're choosing your projects and priorities over them, and people are incredibly sensitive to what appears to be a loss of status. In our attention-starved world, there's even more of a relationship between attention and status than there has been in the past.

For instance, let's say you're working on a project that requires working when your partner wants to focus on her health. Rather than assuming that your partner's doing their thing and you're doing yours, there may be a way that you can exercise with your partner while talking out what's going on with your project.

Or maybe your boss wants you to focus on a different project than the one you're working on. You may be able to do your boss's project but in a way that increases the skills, expertise, contacts, or credibility that can be leveraged for your project.

Weaving OPP into your project isn't always possible, but "How can I weave OPP into my project?" is always a good question to ask. That said, be careful that you don't accommodate or weave OPP into your project so much that it becomes so unwieldy in scope or so difficult to negotiate that you can't finish it. As a rule, projects with fewer people involved tend to be finished faster, but projects fueled by more robust success packs are easier to finish.

The above strategies for handling OPP address the people in your life who are generally supportive of you and what you're working on. Alas, these strategies are inadequate for your derailers and naysayers. We'll turn to them next.

DERAILERS AND NAYSAYERS

If your success pack is the rocket fuel that propels your project, your derailers and naysayers are the winds actively working against you. Not every project has them, but the more your project challenges the status quo, the more likely it is that you'll have some derailers and naysayers. Someone benefits from status quo, and they rarely relinquish those benefits without a strong protest or fight.

But the fact that they work against you doesn't mean that derailers and naysayers are the same thing: derailers are sometimes well-meaning people whose "help" and "feedback" throw you off course, while naysayers are people who are actively against you and your project. It's the difference between a dog that gets too excited and bites you versus a dog that's a biter; the end result is that you're bitten, sure, but you may be able to enjoy being around the too-excited biter.

HOW TO HANDLE DERAILERS

The most challenging thing about derailers is that they often don't know they're derailers. From their perspective, they're trying to help and want you to be successful. From your perspective, you either have to armor up to interact with them or emotionally reset after talking to them.

Your derailer could be your mom, an editor by trade, who proofreads and corrects your online writing without asking. It could be your partner who's the frugal one in your relationship that questions and critiques every purchase you make or are even thinking about making. It could be your uber-successful sibling who thinks your idea is an adorable pet project but isn't worth taking too seriously. In a professional context, it could be an overly critical boss who expects you to have a fully formed idea before you talk to them about it or the "devil's advocate" guy who picks apart your idea without ever evaluating and praising its merits.

Assuming that your derailers are well-meaning and want you to be successful, here's how to go about interacting with them:

1. **Confirm that they want you to be successful with your project.** Sometimes a simple "Hey, I sometimes get the feeling that you don't want me to be successful with this project or idea" is enough to start a good conversation. It's typically not useful for you to have an exhaustive catalogue of the ways they've derailed you, but listing general themes (as I did above) is helpful. In a professional context, you may need to cloak the request as a collaboration technique to depersonalize it. The end goal of this conversation is to get buy-in confirmation and an agreement to try a different way of interacting.

2. **Request the type of feedback or partnership you're looking for.** If you need your partner to *not* critique every purchase for the next few months, put that on the table. If you want the "devil's advocate" guy to evaluate the merits of your idea first, then request that. What rarely works is doing what they do to you back to them; they're better at it than you are, and it may signal that that's how you want to interact. Plus, being passive-aggressive is never a good look.

3. **If they continue to do their derailing thing, don't vote them off the island or put them in the naysayer camp yet.** Remind them of their agreement to try a different approach or "collaboration technique." Your request is likely interrupting deeply ingrained habits or unconscious patterns. Try a three-strike rule before you move to the next strategy.

4. **If they continue to do their derailing thing, your second fallback is to be more strategic about when you have conversations with them.** For instance, it may be better to talk to your fully-formed-idea-first boss after you've run it past your success pack; in this case, you're more likely to get praise for such a well-thought-out idea than criticism for a half-baked idea.

5. **If they continue to derail you after step 4, then follow the suggestion I gave for dealing with OPP you can't accept or reject: do your project covertly and avoid talking about it anymore.** People get tripped up here because they want to celebrate progress or accidentally slip into discussing setbacks vis-à-vis the covert project, but that's the door for the derailer to walk through. If the derailer specifically asks how the project is going, a generic "good" or "it's coming along" is your best bet, even if it's not going well. The only exception to this is in the (very) off chance that their derailing pattern is actually what will help you get unstuck.

I'm fully aware that the steps above look like a lot of work and, yes, it will require courage to have some of the conversations. The payoff is in line with the fact that learning to include rather than sidestep your derailers removes some of the active force against you and your project as well as potentially upgrades them to success pack members.

HOW TO DEAL WITH NAYSAYERS

Naysayers remind me of the parable of the scorpion and the frog. In case you've never heard of it, the scorpion asks the frog to ferry him across the pond. The frog objects, claiming that the scorpion will sting him. But the scorpion replies that it would make no sense to sting the frog. The frog, seeing the reason in the scorpion's argument, relents and lets the scorpion on his back. Midway across the lake, the scorpion stings the frog and, before they both drown, the frog asks why the scorpion stung him. The scorpion's response: "It's in my nature to sting."

For whatever reason, it's the nature of a naysayer to naysay. Singer-songwriter Taylor Swift had it right that "haters gonna hate." Some people are equal-opportunity naysayers and put down everything equally. Some people's naysaying is particular to their relationship with you. Others may feel a responsibility and see their naysaying as vocally and proactively asserting standards.

It's rare that the one naysayer in a thousand people will bear any weight on your success unless you overfocus on them. The exception, of course, is when a naysayer is part of the much smaller circle of people who can approve, reject, or tank your project. If one of your naysayers is on your

It takes .5 seconds from the moment your brain receives unwanted input to the moment you close down or armor up.

But a Wonder Intervention can trip your wiring and open you up to opportunity. A Wonder Intervention is an evidence-based practice that brings more openness and purpose to our work and relationships.

To discover opportunity in a derailer's input, try this:

▶ **Observe and reverse.** Before you react, recalibrate. Rub your temples. Repeat to yourself, "Open up instead of size up." Doing so reverses the closed state both in mind and body.

▶ **Normalize instead of pathologize.** Observe your reaction as a common biological defense and refrain from internal storytelling about the other person or your project. Say something clear and curious to yourself such as, "That's an interesting reaction." No obsessing, please.

▶ **Open to collaborative input.** Ask the person a clarifying question such as, "What prompted your input?" Or "Could you elaborate on X?" Ask them a more open-ended question that could elicit their genuine curiosity versus criticism: "Could you see the project this way?" "What if X happened?"

▶ **Listen with your feet.** Drop awareness to your feet. This prompt lets you receive without defense. Doing so has helped numerous managers, startup founders, creatives, and team players forge wholly different, more productive relationships on behalf of projects greater than their egos.

You would be surprised by what could happen. The derailer suddenly could become an ally, advocate, and ambassador for your project because you shifted the dynamic. It's possible.

Jeffrey Davis is CEO of Tracking Wonder, a consulting firm that equips creatives, leaders, and organizations to brand with integrity. The Wonder Interventions at Work programs help entrepreneurs as well as teams override implicit biases, boost daily creative problem-solving, and foster more open workplaces. A speaker and author of four books, Jeffrey writes for outlets such as *Psychology Today*.

dissertation committee, that's a real problem. Similarly, if your boss or boss's boss is a naysayer, that's a real problem. In the former case, you need to get them off your committee, and, in the latter, you've got to win them over (unlikely) or get out of their chain (probable).[1]

Fortunately it's relatively rare to have a personal naysayer who has that much power over you and your project. What's far more common are the ghost naysayers that we turn into dragons. The only way to beat these kinds of dragons is to realize that they're illusions and projections.

Think about your chosen project. If you've sat with it long enough, you've probably generated some naysayers. The naysayers that are easiest to dismiss are the ones that take some form of anonymous people "out there" (on the internet, in your city, in some cubicle in a galaxy far, far away). If you can't replace the "they" in "What if they don't like it?" with a real name, you've got ghost naysayers. (Try it.)

The second kind of naysayers are actual people who have responded to you or your work. These naysayers are likely people from your past, such as that fifth-grade teacher who embarrassed you by critiquing your writing, or Jimmy from eighth grade who teased you when you couldn't climb the rope. Past naysayers are ghost naysayers at this point; the only power they currently have is what you give them.

When you see ghost naysayers for what they truly are—your own head trash—you're not likely to have many real naysayers to contend with. But in the case where you have real naysayers, here's what to do:

---

1. If your boss is particularly disagreeable, Robert I. Sutton's *The No Asshole Rule: Building a Civilized Workplace and Surviving One That Isn't* (New York: Business Plus, 2010) provides some insights and strategies that are much more relevant to your scenario.

- **Don't engage with them.** No matter what you do and what they say, you'll end up stung and drowning.

- **Stop trying to make them happy or alter your project to meet their approval.** The worst case is that you actually do so, because now you're beholden to pleasing a naysayer and have probably done so by dismissing or neglecting your yaysayers.

- **When you have the urge to engage with a naysayer, engage with a yaysayer instead.** They're in your success pack and probably all around you.

- **In the extremely unlikely case that a naysayer ceases their active naysaying, do not think that they've joined your success pack and you're now BFFs.** They've now been promoted to derailer, at best. Better yet, focus on your yaysayers and success pack, since that's probably what led to you getting the naysayer's approval anyway.

The hardest naysayers to deal with will be people from your nuclear birth family, as you're literally bound to them by blood. Few things cut as deep as naysayer-level rejection by your parents or siblings. The strategies above are just as valid for family naysayers as any other, with the only alteration to the strategies being in the first: don't engage with them about your work. Thanksgiving dinner isn't the time or place to defend your project or work. Follow the covert project strategy from page 162 as well.

> **Every ounce of energy you use grappling with a naysayer is much better spent on working on your project and interacting with your success pack.**

Choose the people who have got your back, not those who never will.

HOW TO DO A PROJECT PREMORTEM

How many times have you sat through a meeting or conversation where you discussed what led to a project going sideways or into the gutter and thought to yourself, "It would've been nice if we had talked about this *before* we kicked off the project"? Or how many times have you realized midproject that, if you had taken a second to think about it, you probably could have avoided or planned for whatever you're now bumping up against?

A project premortem is the process of considering all the ways that a project might go south so you can actively work to prevent those things. Doing a premortem doesn't assume that the project is going to die but rather that every project will have some challenges along the way. Known, planned-for challenges don't tank projects; surprises and willful insanity—repeatedly doing the same thing while expecting that *this time* it's not going to trip you up—do. The converse is true: failing to do the things you know work and wondering why you're struggling is also willful insanity.

Now that you know the universal kinds of drag points and hopefully see that you're not somehow uniquely defective because they plague you, you can make a checklist to walk through your premortem. You neither have to recreate the wheel nor repeatedly climb out of the same hole. Huzzah!

You're doing a premortem at this point because you may need to alter the timeline based on drag points that are likely to come up. For instance, if you accidentally put a derailer in your success pack—it's really easy to do—subbing them out for someone who's more supportive or placing them later in the process may alter how long something will take. If you baked in OPP in your estimate as to how long something would take but now see that you may be able to co-opt the person, you may alter the timeline or build in some additional time because, while it may take longer to do, best-work projects are better with friends and loved ones.

Let's return to your project. Though we've been discussing drag points and ways your project can go sideways on you, let's refocus on the fact that you've picked an idea that matters to you, converted that idea into a SMART goal, and assembled a success pack that will help you stay on course. You already have what it takes to be successful, and what you might lack now you can acquire on the journey. (It's important to do premortems from a grounded, resilient, and positive perspective.)

Now use the following questions to do your project premortem:

▸ Have you created any no-win scenarios for yourself? How might you detangle them?

▸ Have you picked a method of doing your project that's especially hard for you? How might you *start from* and leverage your GATES?

▸ What OPP do you need to account for? How might you align OPP with your project?

▸ Are there any derailers and (real) naysayers you need to account for? List them by name and how you'll address them.

▸ Are you carrying any projects that you can let go of to keep them from bogging you down?

▸ Are there any bad or unhelpful stories you're telling yourself—you're a flake, you're not good at planning, who are you to think you can do it, and others—and what will you do to counteract those stories?

If you're honestly engaging with the questions above, you're likely to have a range of emotions that vacillate between feeling daunted to feeling eager to overcome your drag points. If you're mostly feeling daunted and overwhelmed, great! Sit with it and return to your premortem after a few days, as you'll likely have generated some solutions and breakthroughs when you return. If you're mostly feeling eager to overcome your drag points, great! Do a metaphorical victory lap and know that we're going to get nitty-gritty in the next chapter about getting your project on your schedule.

CHAPTER 7 TAKEAWAYS

▶ Drag points are the natural places where reality will push against your plans.

▶ There are three kinds of no-win scenarios we often tell ourselves: the Success Will Wreck My Relationships tale, the Success Versus Virtue myth, and the What If I Can't Do It Again? trap.

▶ We choose mediocrity (in the short term) because we don't want to succeed due to the no-win scenarios but we also don't want to fail—mediocrity is the space between success and failure.

▶ OPP (other people's priorities) create conflict with our best work, but there are often ways to weave OPP into our work and convert conflict into cooperation.

▶ Derailers are well-meaning people whose "help" and "feedback" throw you off course; naysayers are people who are actively against you and your project.

▶ Project premortems help identify and avoid the challenges that may kill or slow your projects.

PART 3

WORKING THE PLAN

Don't be fooled by the calendar. There are only
as many days in the year as you make use of.
CHARLES RICHARDS

WEAVE YOUR PROJECT INTO YOUR SCHEDULE

The weekly block schedule, the Five Projects Rule, and your
project road map together create a plan you can follow and
space to do the work. Addressing the natural drag points also
helps make sure you use the space and plan you have to do
the work.

To start doing your best work, you have to start weaving
your project into your total work-life schedule, and reality
will start defying your best-laid plans as soon as you lay them.
When your plans and reality don't match, the only sensible
choice is to adjust your plans. It's counterintuitive, but the
better planner you are, the more often you'll review and
adjust your plans.

Momentum planning is my term for the continual process
of making and adjusting plans across all time perspectives.
It incorporates well-worn practices such as weekly reviews,
morning planning, and triaging, but it also weaves in time
blocking, the project pyramid, and the Five Projects Rule.
But now that we're talking about reality's effects on your
plans, it's time to consider whether the reality you're working
in is working for you.

MAKE SURE YOUR ENVIRONMENT IS WORKING FOR YOU

When I was in graduate school and found myself unable to write, I'd go to my secret writing place: Love Library at the University of Nebraska–Lincoln. Love Library has some half-level floors that are rarely used, but these floors still have desks that look out toward the capitol. In the near stillness amid the smell of old books and journal articles, I'd open up Mellel (at the time, the best writing app for academics), turn on some background classical music, and write for hours. It was reliable enough that a week before the deadline, I could review my research notes, do last-minute reading (or all the reading) up until three days before the deadline, write for a day, edit it the next day, and send it on the deadline.

But if I tried the same thing *without* going to the library, my plans for meeting the deadline would all fall apart on me. The pressure of the deadlines meant that I could force myself through a long night of writing at home, but it was torturous and never produced my best work because I'm a lark (more on that later). While it feels odd to admit that all of the writing I did in the seven-odd years I spent in graduate school was probably done in less than sixty days of focused writing, it was the same for many of my peers.

A dozen years and a few hundred thousand words later, I know that it would have been much smarter to just go to the library twice per week—probably on Monday and Tuesday—ready to write. That's wisdom that young adults and creative amateurs can't hear, though.

But you're much smarter and ready than I was at the time, and you probably know how important environment is for your focus, momentum, and creativity. You've also experienced what it's like for your best-laid plan for the day to go sideways because your chatty coworkers distracted you all day or the construction crew started next door on the day you had allotted for quiet writing. The question is whether you're actively creating the space for you to do your best work—like Tony Stark.

While I could wax on about how the first *Iron Man* movie was a watershed moment for me, what's relevant for our present conversation is the way Tony Stark's lab was set up for him to be able to build his high-tech power suits. He'd touch a virtual screen, swipe to the left, tell the computer to add different components and materials, and then the robots would spin and whir in the background to build the myriad ideas he just put in the queue. Tony Stark's lab was custom-made to capture his ideas with as little friction as possible and then start making whatever he wanted with as little work for him as possible.

That is the ideal, and though you may not be one of the smartest and richest people in a fictional universe, knowing what your lab—or workshop, sanctuary, kitchen, or whatever metaphor most resonates with you—would look like is a powerful way to work backward to an environment that works for you. If your lab would have big windows to let the sunlight and seaside vista come in, you know that your desk in the corner of the basement is temporary and that it may be time to get some beach posters and better lighting.

The following are some environmental factors to consider when thinking about whether your environment works for you:

▶ **Sound.** Consider coworkers talking in the background, the sounds of a coffee shop, the buzz of children playing in the distance, the hum of the ceiling fan, the babbling of a brook, or the hustle-bustle of a busy city street. Each sound affects us differently. Figure out what background noise best serves your best work.

▶ **Smell.** It's obvious that disgusting smells can make it hard to focus, but there may be smells that really get you in the zone. Of all the senses, our sense of smell brings us closest to our memory center,[1] so smells can have a powerful effect on getting us in the zone.

▶ **Sunlight.** Studies show that sunlight affects our moods,[2] and there's a right amount for each of us. Night owls often prefer working in darker rooms.

▶ **Clothing.** Yes, what you wear is a part of your environment and is worth considering. Pants that don't fit in all the wrong places can be distracting, as can itchy socks. It's also true that you may not take yourself or your work seriously if you're working in your pajamas and a shirt you've been wearing for the last three days. It may also be that those pajamas and shirt make up your lucky outfit. If it works for you, I'm not judging.

1. Amanda White, "Smells Ring Bells: How Smell Triggers Memories and Emotions," *Psychology Today*, January 12, 2015, psychologytoday.com/us/blog/brain-babble/201501/smells-ring-bells-how-smell-triggers-memories-and-emotions.

2. Alice Park, "Why Sunlight Is So Good For You," *Time*, August 7, 2017, time.com/4888327/why-sunlight-is-so-good-for-you.

▸ **Clutter/Organization.** It's not necessarily true for everyone that a clean desk equates to a clean mind, as I've witnessed people who can't focus with a clean desk or in a Zen/spartan environment. Your tolerance for clutter or tidiness may also depend on the space in question.

▸ **Amount of space.** Some people like the coziness of small rooms with lots of furniture, shelves, and so on, whereas others prefer more spacious rooms with less furniture. Like clutter, it could also be that only parts of your work area need to be spacious. Even further, it could be that certain kinds of stuff in your space create different feelings for you.

▸ **Music.** While studies show that listening to classical music increases focus and creativity,[3] you may not be able to concentrate with it. It may be that certain kinds of music work for you or *really* don't work for you, or the level of music makes a lot of difference. For instance, I typically can't do focus blocks while listening to music with spoken words, but the "This Is Coheed and Cambria" playlist on Spotify has been in the background for much of the drafting of this book; Jack Johnson radio on Spotify powers my admin blocks. Coheed and Cambria is an uncharacteristic choice, but it just works. Your best-work music may be similarly variable and unusual.

---

3. "Can Music Help You Study and Focus?" Northcentral University (website), March 29, 2017, ncu.edu/blog/can-music-help-you-study-and-focus#gref.

Work—whether it's paid work or volunteer work or creative work—is a big part of what we're here for on this earth. It builds the dignity of self-reliance in us at the same time it satisfies our generous instincts by utilizing our skills and talents to help others.

Minimalism maximizes our potential—work included. Choosing to focus our time on endeavors that matter is important. Additionally, clearing physical clutter (external chaos) from our workspace increases our potential.

Some of us have the idea that a messy, crowded office typifies a busy, productive worker. "My office is a mess, but I know where everything is" is a common mantra. We pile papers, folders, notes, and books on our desk almost as if we wear our clutter as a badge of honor.

Unfortunately, more often than not, a messy office typifies a disorganized, unfocused, stressed-out worker who is running behind and out of control. A cluttered workspace doesn't contribute to meaningful work, it distracts us from it.

When you free up space in your work environment (whatever that may be for you), you'll feel more at peace and be able to do your work more efficiently. You'll find that you've freed up your mind to think clearer and deeper, make decisions better, and plan further ahead. Rather than working at the mercy of the business and busyness of modern-day life, you'll be more proactive about your future.

Clearing clutter turns our environment into one that helps us get more and better work done with less stress. More than that, it might actually transform the legacy we leave.

Joshua Becker is the bestselling author of *The Minimalist Home: A Room-by-Room Guide to a Decluttered, Refocused Life* and *The More of Less: Finding the Life You Want Under Everything You Own.* He is also the founder and editor of BecomingMinimalist.com, a website inspiring others to live more by owning less.

The recurring theme is that what works or doesn't work in your environment is unique to your preferences. Approach this as if you're Tony Stark. While you're considering what in your environment might not be working for you, you can also consider what it would look like for your environment to be optimal for you.

Making your environment work for you may come down to moving to a different location rather than changing what's in your location.

You may find that going to a coffee shop, library, or the unused conference room for your focus blocks is the best way to do your best work, but why you do so is probably because of one of the factors I mentioned. This may be especially true if you work in an open-plan office. Luckily we're trending away from open-plan offices in favor of the hub-and-spoke model based on evidence that the open-plan office environment isn't conducive for focused, deep work.[4]

Depending on how poorly or well your environment is working for you, making it work for you could be its own project, which also means you have to watch out for it being a convenient excuse to avoid doing your best work.

It's a matter of taking the steps, large and small, to make your environment ever closer to Tony Stark's lab. And yes, sometimes it's as simple as going to the coffee shop or hiding away in unused levels of a library.

---

4. Geoffrey James, "Open-Plan Offices Kill Productivity, According to Science," *Inc.*, May 18, 2017, inc.com/geoffrey-james/science-just-proved-that-open-plan-offices-destroy-productivity.html.

BATCHING AND STACKING WORK INCREASES YOUR EFFICIENCY

Thinking about where you work and how it's working for you naturally leads you to consider what kinds of activities you might do in different places and contexts. For instance, if you need to print and review your work, working from a coffee shop or airplane will be inefficient. If you're organizing a community event, it may make more sense to do a lot of the required prep work at the physical location of the event. Or if you're out running one errand, it may be more efficient to do multiple errands at once.

Batching and stacking are strategies that help you work more efficiently. *Batching* is the process of doing similar kinds of work in a contiguous stretch of time. *Stacking* is the process of doing dissimilar kinds of work in the same stretch of time.

Batching is easier to explain and what you're probably already doing, so we'll start there, using processing email as an example. You *could* check and process[5] one email at a time, then switch to something else, and then switch back, but it would be horribly inefficient. It takes us sixteen minutes to refocus after fielding incoming email.[6] You would spend a third to half of your day refocusing and transitioning. (Yes, many people do spend their days in a digital fog.)

In this case, it's clear that processing multiple emails at once is more efficient; you're already there and in that mode, so you may as well knock out a few at once and *then* transition back to focused work. Batching is already baked into the concept of

---

5. I'm using *process* rather than *check* email because checking email is something we need to do far less of. If you practice only going to email when you intend to process it, then you won't be touching email multiple times needlessly.

6. "You Waste a Lot of Time at Work," Atlassian, accessed January 24, 2019, atlassian.com/time-wasting-at-work-infographic.

admin blocks, because while you're in an admin block, you're likely going to triage and process admin tasks.

Batching works so well because it minimizes the context shifting and mental or physical back-and-forth that can occur when we jump from context to context. It prevents the waste that would happen if we, say, went to our physical mailbox multiple times per day to retrieve or place one piece of mail rather than going once to retrieve and place all our mail. It's great for errands, chores, admin work (transactional calls, email, filing, etc.), and organization.

On the surface, stacking appears to be multitasking, but multitasking is a troublesome concept and, if done unreflectively, actually leads to distraction and inefficiency because most of what people call multitasking is actually rapid refocusing, to use productivity coach and bestselling author David Allen's appropriate term. Jumping from email, to social media, to your calendar, to a website, to a different tab, back to email quickly zaps your cognitive juice at the same time that it primes you for more clicking. A day of clicking is rarely a day of getting your best work done.

What distinguishes stacking from batching is that it uses different kinds of physical and mental resources simultaneously. A few easy examples of task stacking are:

▹ Doing laundry while listening to an audiobook
▹ Doing an audio or real-time meeting while hiking
▹ Exercising in the park while spending time with the kids

In the first two examples, muscle memory is doing most of the physical work, so there's open cognitive bandwidth to do other things. For the third, it's possible to keep an eye on the kids and/or include them while exercising.

It's when you're doing things that require mental or physical focus that you need to watch out. Checking email while doing deep writing doesn't work very well, as does having a focused conversation while trying to do deep reading. While stacking might seem to redefine multitasking, the point of using a different term is to (a) break the habit or disrupt the belief of trying to do inefficient multitasking, and (b) have you think about the kinds of activities that you *can* do well simultaneously.

KEEP THE DREAD-TO-WORK RATIO DOWN BY DEALING WITH FROGS EARLIER AND EVERY DAY

While we're on batching and stacking and energy drain, it's time to address frogs, which you'll recall are the things we really don't want to do. It's amazing how some of the smallest tasks can take on lives of their own. Of course, the truth is that they don't take on lives of their own—*we* are the ones that give them their vitality.

A frog could be something as simple as paying a bill, even though we have the money to pay. Or it could be responding to an email that might take three minutes to do, if we'd just make up our mind and do it.

Mark Twain was dead-on with this: "If you know you have to swallow a frog, swallow it first thing in the morning. If there are two frogs, swallow the big one first."[7] You swallow the frog first thing in the morning so that you can avoid increasing the *dread-to-work* ratio of your day.

---

7. After I wrote about frogs in 2008, I learned about Brian Tracy's *Eat That Frog! 21 Ways to Stop Procrastinating and Get More Done in Less Time* (Oakland, CA: Berrett-Koehler, 2006). This is a case of independent codevelopment from the same inspiration.

THE DREAD-TO-WORK RATIO, EXPLAINED

Most tasks generally require a fixed minimum amount of work, meaning that doing them later won't make them any easier. If a task was going to take five minutes at first, then odds are it's going to take at least five minutes *whenever* you do it. The "work" part of the equation stays the same.

It's the "dread" that increases substantially with time. The longer the task sits there, the more you think about it; the amount of time you've invested in thinking about and putting off the task somehow gets added to the psychological size of the task. The frog gets bigger and wartier, and the warts themselves start growing hairs and warts. It feels that way, at least.

After a while, the distinction between *directly* working on that task and *indirectly* working on it blurs to the point at which it doesn't make sense to make the distinction. If you've spent all day (or week) avoiding and fretting about the task, then you've spent time and energy on it that you could have spent on other things. To think about it in terms of the soft costs of inaction belies the point that it's still costly.

A FROG A DAY KEEPS YOUR ANCHORS AWEIGH

My prior suggestion to catch the frog first thing in the morning isn't quite fine-grained enough. Just as with time, not all frogs are the same. A frog that requires a creative solution to address may require a focus block. When a bunch of little frogs can be caught at the same time, they should be batched and caught together. But be honest with yourself about whether you're putting off catching your frogs because you have a more effective plan or because you really don't want to catch them.

As a general strategy to keep momentum going, identify your frogs and catch at least one a day. When you do this, three interrelated effects occur:

▸ You keep your dread-to-work ratio lower because you identify your frogs early on, acknowledge them for what they are, and swallow them sooner rather than later.

▸ You get fewer and smaller frogs because you start thinking about the nature of your frogs and see trends and patterns in your workflow. Once you see those trends and patterns, you can start eliminating or minimizing the parts of your life and work that generate those frogs in the first place.

▸ You start the momentum spiral that I mentioned previously because you release a lot of the energy held up in not working on frogs while at the same time having fewer of them. That reclaimed energy and time can be spent on your best work.

But I should be clear here: there will always be frogs. They may be smaller, they may come up less often, and they may be an entirely new type of frog, but they'll pop up nonetheless. "Do you have any frogs?" is thus not the question but rather "Where are the frogs you need to address?"

Spot 'em, weave addressing them into your day, and move on to the next thing. There's no need to increase the work by dreading it so much.

WHEN BEFORE WHAT

Addressing frogs opens the door for us to consider more pattern-level considerations around when to do certain kinds of work. Many people buy a ticket to ride the struggle bus for a week before the week even begins because they start their plans with *what* needs to be done rather than looking strategically at *when* it's better to do it. But we need to look more narrowly and more broadly than just the week, as there are better and worse times during the day and during the year to work on projects.

Before we get too far down this road, though, do not be lulled into thinking that figuring out when to do your best work is a magic pill. Just as it's a trap to keep waiting until you have empty days and weeks to work on what matters, it's a trap to believe that all it takes is an ideal schedule for you to start making progress. At best, planning to do the work during the right times removes barriers that make progress harder—you won't be fighting dragons when your energy and resolve are the lowest. That said, you want to create all the advantages you can.

TIME OF DAY

There's no shortage of admonition and advice to get up early and focus on first things first, with little regard for the reality that humans have three chronotypes, defined as "the individual propensity for sleep and activity at particular times during a twenty-four-hour period."[8] The ubiquitous exhortation to be early birds (larks) attempts to shoehorn the night owls and afternoon emus,[9] but a person's true chronotype only seems to change with age.

While it's typically the case that the Industrial Revolution's paradigms don't fit us, in this case, the standard three factory shifts do reasonably well. Alas,

---

8. David N. Samson et al., "Chronotype Variation Drives Night-Time Sentinel-Like Behavior in Hunter-Gatherers," *Proceedings of the Royal Society: Biological Sciences* 284, no. 1858 (July 12, 2017): dx.doi.org/10.1098/rspb.2017.0967.

9. Daniel Pink calls emus "third birds" in *When: The Scientific Secrets of Perfect Timing* (New York: Riverhead Books, 2018), but I'm calling them "emus" because I think the group deserves their own bird name. Emus are also odd birds out when they're defined in contrast to flying birds.

many creatives now work in standard nine-to-five environments, and even when we don't work in co-located buildings, we're expected to be "on" during those hours. Just as the workday is wrapping up, emus may just be getting in their creative peak and owls may be approaching their warm-up.

Your boss may have a strong influence on your timing and availability, but if you're an independent creative, it's often better to shift your schedule to match your chronotype than try to shift your chronotype to match people's preferences. Most creative people are far more capable of shifting and creating their schedule than it at first seems—it's more often lack of awareness and courage than possibility. Our education system and work cultures normalize us to be larks to the degree that people often don't know they're not larks or give themselves permission to explore emu or owl schedules; when they become aware and give themselves permission to work on their natural schedules, there's often a series of conversations to be had that require courage to see through.

For instance, many lark creative mothers spend what would otherwise be their most creative times waking up their kids and getting them to school. One option for reclaiming the morning might be to ask their partner to be the kid wrangler; another might be to negotiate with the family to go to bed earlier so they can get up earlier, in which case the kid-wrangling occurs after their focus block and serves as a postcreative incubation cycle. Emus might prefer their mornings to start with meetings, so they free up their afternoons for focused work, but doing so may also mean negotiating no-meeting afternoons with coworkers and colleagues. Owls may follow a similar strategy with the afternoons being their social time, so they have the evenings and nights free.

MIKE VARDY   YOU DON'T HAVE TO BE AN EARLY RISER TO BE PRODUCTIVE

I've got a little secret to share with you: you don't have to be an early riser to be productive. You don't have to be a morning person to get ahead of the game. In fact, it's more important if you're someone who works better in the later hours of the day to avoid the allure of trying to be a morning person instead of paying attention to your natural tendencies as a night owl.

Why?

You have bigger battles to fight—such as taking care of your to-do list—and spending energy on changing your body clock isn't the best use of your time and attention. Instead, focus on being proactive in a different way than your early-rising counterparts . . . like I do.

Here are two quick tips to thrive as a night owl in a world geared toward early risers:

▶ Flip the script and do your big tasks later to stay proactive, and do your easier tasks in the early part of your day so that you save your best self for your prime working hours.

▶ Make sure you have both a morning *and* evening routine. In fact, I'd say your evening routine is more important than your morning because having it in place allows you to start off the next day with less friction.

It's okay to be a night owl. I've made it work for years, and if you follow the simple steps above, you can make it work for you too.

Mike Vardy is a writer, a productivity strategist, and the founder of TimeCrafting. He is the author of several books, including *The Front Nine: How to Start the Year You Want Anytime You Want* and *The Productivityist Playbook*. He is a renowned speaker and has taught productivity practices on the popular online education platforms CreativeLive and Skillshare, where his courses are among the most popular in the business category. Mike lives in Victoria, British Columbia, Canada, with his incredible wife, daughter, and son.

As you're thinking through when might be the best time of day for you to do your best work, realize that people don't know what's on your schedule and will often assume that you have other commitments driving your availability. I bring this up because a lot of people approach the schedule-making process as if they need to defend their unavailability. But unless you tell people or you have entirely too-limited availability, your unavailability rarely comes up. So rather than making your focus blocks fit around other people's schedules, set your focus blocks as the default that others need to work around. Unless everyone you work with is the same chronotype as you and have expressed incompatible schedules, you're likely to find times that work for everyone.

DAY OF THE WEEK

Some days of the week may be better to do certain kinds of work than other days. For instance, you may find that Monday is a great day for planning and getting caught up with your work, so you can batch meetings and work to be focused on getting the week started off right; doing this on Friday may not work nearly as well if you and your team are checking out. Or maybe Monday is a particularly challenging day to do any heavy lifting because your ex has the kids for the weekend and there's emotional fallout Sunday evening and the next morning, so it makes more sense for Monday to be more focused on admin and self-care.

While it's true that your work context and level of autonomy will vary, you can still set yourself up for success by thinking through what days of the week are best for certain kinds of work.

Here are some general principles:

▷ **Put the work that requires the most effort—decisions, analysis and evaluation, and deep work—on the days when you have the most creative, positive energy.** Those days should have the most focus blocks as well; having more focus blocks on the days when you have the best energy for them provides a useful default that will aid your momentum planning. For many people, Mondays and Tuesdays make the most sense, though it may take some work to clear up those days from routine meetings and the Monday-morning busywork mindset.

▷ **Batch follow-up and collaborative work for the days when more people are available and "in the zone."** Again, for most people, this is Tuesday through Thursday. Sending check-in and heavy-thought emails on Monday morning and Friday afternoon just increases the likelihood that the receivers will punt the emails and calls.

▷ **Schedule "lighter" social meetings on Thursday and Friday.** By light, I mean conversations that are mostly about rapport-building and relationship maintenance more than major decision-making, strategy discussions, or coworking. Thursdays and Fridays are also great for weekly reviews and checkouts with your coworkers or success pack, since those events tend to create deadlines that focus attention for the week.

The overlap in the days above reflects reality, and how you arrange your blocks in the days will allow you to address multiple goals. For instance, if you're a lark and a Monday seizer, Monday and Tuesday mornings may be focus blocks just for your best work; Monday and Tuesday afternoons may feature meetings that require a lot of braining and energy to get through, and you may also make sure your admin blocks in the afternoons on those days are for follow-ups and check-ins. In this scenario, you can bet your Fridays are going to need to be much less intense and demanding, so you can have your networking, checkouts, and admin work scheduled then.

Weekends are your wildcards. While I've advanced the hegemony of the Monday-through-Friday workweek,[10] it's just a social convention. It's a powerful one, for sure, but

there's no necessary reason that you can't claim parts or all of Saturday and Sunday for your best work.

In fact, Saturday and Sunday are often the very best days for people to do their best work because many of us don't have professional distractions and interruptions—our coworkers are less likely to interrupt us if they're not actually working.

With the idea that Saturday and Sunday are possible work days, we can take it one step further: there's no reason that Monday has to be the "start" of the week. Many people are frustrated that their Mondays are so full of busywork and they're already behind and unable to do their best work for the week. But if Sunday is the day you get your best work or weekly planning done—and you do that work—then you're already on track for the week. You've done your first things first just by changing what day you mark as first.

An important caveat here is to remember to schedule time to rest. I recommend at least one day per week for my clients—which is often a fight in the first place—but two or three might be what you need because, after all, your work isn't the *only* thing you've got going. The exception here is when clients are on sprints, project pushes, or in a high

---

10. This is the European hegemony; the Arab workweek is Sunday through Thursday, with Friday and Saturday off.

season that's just part of their work cycles, but the constant sprint–push–high-season pattern is the road to burnout.

While we're on reclaiming the weekends, many creative parents or caretakers overlook the reality that they could get sitters or caretakers during the weekend *days* just as well as the *evenings*. If you're a lark or emu who's also a parent or caretaker, having a sitter watch the kids on a Saturday while you're going after it at home or at the office can be a powerful way to make progress on your best work, and it's honestly a far better bang for your buck. Would you rather pay fifteen dollars an hour for a sitter to watch movies with your kids in the evening or pay that same fifteen dollars an hour to have them take your kids to the park and then *you* get to watch the movies and have dinner with the kids after having the satisfaction of getting your work done? (Yes, you may now be thrashing with competing priorities in a different way; this is also why we made a project budget.)

With some weekly schedule calibration and mindset changes, you can stop being resigned at the end of the week or anxious that you're behind at the start of the week. Remember: when reality doesn't fit your plans (schedule), don't try to change reality—change your plans.

You could take this idea of timing further by considering seasons of the year. You may be naturally inspired and have more best-work energy in the winter but be sluggish in the summer. Or maybe spring is when it's best for you to kick off new major projects. And, obviously, if your best work requires you to be outdoors or is tied to the natural seasons, factor that into your project road maps and the Five Projects Rule.

"FIRST THINGS FIRST" ISN'T NECESSARILY ABOUT SEQUENCE

"First things first" is a reminder to make sure that you're taking action on your most important priorities rather than letting less important stuff eat up your time. That's straightforward enough, but it often leads to an inference that the most important priorities should be attended to before other things *in sequence.*

That's not necessarily the case. First in *priority* doesn't mean first in *sequence.*

For instance, if your top priority is to do your creative work, but you're not a morning person, then it's probably better for you to focus on noncreative work in the morning so that you're not trying to do creative work at the wrong time of the day.

Similarly, your most important project for this quarter might fruitfully be delayed until you've cleared the deck of other urgent and noisy projects, so you can focus on that big, important project without a cacophony of chattering monkeys in the back of your mind, screaming at you about the other projects.

Or perhaps you've determined that getting the right champions behind your project is the single most important priority to ensure the success of your project, in which case you might need to complete an initial project blueprint *before* you approach those champions.

If you've been frustrated about the things that matter most to you not being the first things you get to—in a day, week, or month—it's all good. What's more important is whether you're getting to those first things at the right time.

WHEN TO DO YOUR MOMENTUM PLANNING

While we're discussing when to do what kinds of work, you might be wondering when you should be doing your planning. Before we get into when might be the best time to create your plan, it's important to remember that the best time to create a plan is when you realize you don't have one. It doesn't matter if it's midday, midweek, or midmonth—if you're scrambling and feel like you're falling behind, you can stop scrambling for fifteen minutes or an hour and get your plan on. Please don't fall into the trap of thinking that just because you didn't start the day, week, or month with a plan that you should tread water until the start of the next day, week, or month.

To address when to do your momentum planning, though, we have to cover frequency. Luckily that's the most straightforward aspect of the practice. Once a week, create your weekly plan. Once a day, create your daily plan. And so on.

If you're in a groove with your momentum planning, it typically doesn't take that long to plan because of the Five Projects Rule.

Here's what tends to work well for people:

▸ **Daily planning—the night before or the first thing in the morning before checking email.** Making your plan before checking email helps prevent OPP from driving your plan. This can typically be done in less than fifteen minutes.

▸ **Weekly planning—Sunday night or first thing Monday morning before checking email.** This can typically be done in less than thirty minutes.

▸ **Monthly planning—the weekend before the month starts or the first Monday of the month.** This may require a focus block if you haven't been doing your weekly momentum planning.

▸ **Quarterly planning—the week before the quarter starts.** Quarterly planning often takes multiple passes if you haven't been doing your monthly momentum planning.

▸ **Annual planning—the month before the year starts.** Annual planning may take multiple passes.

While the presentation above is bottom-up, the reality is that it's *much* easier to do the lower-level momentum planning if you've done the higher-level momentum planning. Knowing what five projects you're working on this month and what recurring projects need to be woven into this week makes it pretty clear what you need to focus on each day.

Additionally, if you did last week's momentum planning, it's pretty simple to figure out what projects you might do this week because of how projects are linked and sequenced. Frequent plotting and course correction (at the right level of perspective) makes it a lot easier to do so.

USE THE 5/10/15 SPLIT TO BUILD DAILY MOMENTUM

The *5/10/15 split* makes your momentum planning a breeze and helps you course correct when reality pushes against your plans. It fuses the Five Projects Rule with the daily frequency of momentum planning. You use your five projects (for the day and week) to create and update your daily plan for ten minutes in the morning and fifteen minutes at the end of the day.

The magic of the 5/10/15 split is that it helps us navigate the two challenges we all have: (1) getting a great start on the day, and (2) letting go at the end of the day.

These two challenges are intimately related. Since we often don't know what we should be doing, we get involved in a lot of easy-to-engage-in tasks that often aren't the things that matter the most. By the time we get our heads on straight, we've squandered a lot of time, so we end up trying to overcompensate by working longer.

Then, at exactly the point at which it's clear that we're no longer able to do something without messing it up, we remember all the stuff we should've been doing in the first place. We know that it won't get done no matter how hard we beat ourselves up about it, yet we also can't just let it go.

Here's the deal:

unless you're good at planning your day, it's really hard to do it first thing in the morning.

It's much easier to check email and get distracted with OPP, which only serves to repeat the same pattern that you're trying to interrupt.

So instead of trying it that way, work on the 10 and 15 parts of the split. The 5 part is the Five Projects Rule, and since you're familiar with that, you can constrain your focus to the weekly and daily perspectives—that is, what are your five projects for this week, and based on that, how you'll spend your blocks to fuel those projects.

The key to getting the 5/10/15 split going is actually the evening checkout rather than the morning check-in. That's why it gets a bit more time, but it's also because you're asking harder questions. We'll start by talking about the checkout.

THE 15-MINUTE CHECKOUT

The checkout is critical because we usually have a better perspective at the end of the day than at the beginning of the day. We know what we did and didn't do, and we have a good idea of the next steps we need to take to keep the ball rolling. So while our level of overwhelm might be higher, we don't suffer the mental cobwebs that cloud the beginning of the day.

The *15-minute checkout* has three questions:

1 What did you accomplish? (Celebrate!) Acknowledge what you did rather than just focusing on what you didn't do. Always, always, *always* celebrate what you accomplished. Life is but a series of small steps, and if you don't celebrate the small wins, it's harder to build up the momentum for the bigger ones.

2 Is there anything that you need to do right now to be able to disengage? This question answers that nagging feeling that you've forgotten to do something. Check your inbox and your to-do list for those things that have to happen today. Ask yourself what would really happen if you didn't do whatever you're considering—you would be surprised how many things can wait until the next day.

3 When do you need to do the things that you didn't get done today? There might be a lot of things that came up during the day that need to get done sometime soon, but they don't have to happen today. If something needs to happen tomorrow or some specific day in the future, put it in whatever app, tool, planner, or calendar you use so that you'll see it tomorrow. That way your mind can let it go and you can get some peace.

If you didn't finish whatever you were working on today, make a note of where to start for the next time you pick it up. This is great for those creative projects on which you need to maintain momentum but that you might not be able to work on every day.

THE 10-MINUTE CHECK-IN

If you start the 5/10/15 split with the 15-minute checkout, you've done most of the hard work. All you have to do next is show up and do what you told yourself you were going to do.

Here are the questions to ask yourself during the *10-minute check-in*:

1 **Has anything significant changed between now and the last checkout?** The key word here is *significant*. Some events do change the course of your day. For instance, your kids might get sick and you'll need to change your plans to be able to take care of them.

2 **What did you plan for today?** This is where you review the plan you made for yourself the day before. Remember, you probably had a better idea of what you need to do today when you did your checkout than you do right now.

3 **What's one thing you're going to start on right now?** This step is all about setting the intention to focus on this one thing for your next block rather than shuffling through a few projects and not making any real progress on any of them. Better to complete or make some real progress on one thing than shuffle through three.

You might be tempted to answer the first question by checking email and voicemail, but before you do, ask yourself what's in there that would change your day. Did you start scheduling something? Are you waiting for something that's related to a project you're working on this morning? Plan on how you're going to process email and voicemail; at this stage, it's best to look for a few key messages that are relevant to what you need to do right now rather than just jumping on to check email.

You might be wondering why it's a 5/10/15 split and not a 5/10/10 or 5/15/15 split. It's a 5/10/15 split because I've learned through trial and error—personally, and with clients and students—that it's a good balance between not giving yourself enough time and requiring too much time. It's hard to get the right level of perspective and thoroughness in less than ten or fifteen minutes, and much longer than that makes it just another thing to resist.

The 5/10/15 split makes every other level of momentum planning that much easier and quicker. Since you're never that far from the guide rails that are your plans, you don't have to struggle to get back to them. And since it's more likely that you have been staying focused on your five projects, there's not a lot of gymnastics and recalibration.

DON'T PLAN OUT TOO FAR IN ADVANCE

Another seemingly counterintuitive practice with momentum planning is intentionally *not* planning further out than you need to. Planning too far out is an excusable way to avoid doing the work that needs to be done *today*—some of us like the puzzle-solving aspect of planning more than rolling up our sleeves and getting the work done.

There's an obvious tension here, though, because not planning out far enough in advance can lead to being underprepared and asking for support too late in the process. For instance, realizing that it would be beneficial to have some of your peers (from your success pack) review an aspect of your project three days before your deadline will make it really hard to get the support you might otherwise need. But the flip side of the coin here is that letting them know you'll need them to look over something in four months *before* you know how the project is progressing may mean you must let them know that you're behind, if you get off track.

Assuming you've accounted for deadlines and relay time and have them captured at the monthly level of planning, four weeks tends to be about as far out as you can reasonably plan daily blocks with any degree of confidence. The project pyramid is your friend here, because, say, three weeks out, you only need to know what week-sized chunk you need to be working on; when it's time to do the momentum planning for that week, you can get into the details of how you're going to use your blocks for that week.

It should be clear that I'm using *plan* in a very specific way: it's not that you don't have *any* idea of what you're going to be doing in the future but that you haven't gotten into a level of detail that will require overadjusting your plans because they're too detailed. As an analogy, if you're making a transcontinental road trip, planning out every bathroom, meal, and fuel break for the next week is overkill. You really only need to know what's ahead of you for the next day.

With practice, you'll find your unique Goldilocks level of advance planning that works best for you. Most of the time, I find that having a good idea of the next two weeks' worth of projects is enough for me to keep things moving without overplanning. At the team level, having a good idea of the next two months' projects (at that time perspective) is enough for me to guide the team and ensure that work they need from me is on my plan. But keep in mind my next two weeks' worth of work is tied to the context of the bigger picture—I may have blinders on, but I know I'm running in the right direction on the right track.

HOW TO DO YOUR FIRST ROUND OF MOMENTUM PLANNING

The 5/10/15 split is a great framework to use to tie your days together, but it doesn't show you the bigger picture. The hardest part of momentum planning is doing the first round, because it's not completely obvious where to start.

Here's a quick rundown of how to do your momentum planning if you're starting from scratch:

1 **Start with the month-level perspective.** It's big enough for context but small enough to not require planning a time to plan.

2 **Review and capture any deadlines or major events.** A major event at the monthly level is usually something that will pull you out of your normal routine for a few days or a one-day event that will require significant preparation; major presentations, weddings, travel that requires four or more days, first or last days of school/work, and move in/out days are all examples of major events at the month-level perspective. These deadlines and events create hard constraints on your schedule and influence both how many blocks you have and what you need to dedicate to them.

3 **If you have a good picture of your five projects for the quarter, review, adjust, and capture them.** These five projects give you the context to determine what your five projects for this month should be.

4 **Decide what your five projects for the month need to be.** Remember that the Five Projects Rule is *technically* no more than five active projects per time perspective, so you don't need to fill up those five project slots—you may not be able to, given step 2 above—and you're committing to *doing* projects rather than just writing them down. It may be helpful to review the action verbs in chapter 5 to figure out which verbs you need to use for your five projects.

5 **Chunk those five projects into week-sized chunks for every week of the month.** Some projects may not need to be spread out over the full month; for instance, if one of your deadlines is to complete an important report, you may decide to spend a few blocks the week prior to its deadline to get it done and reviewed by your colleagues, so it may not need a full slot the week it's due. Remember to apply the Five Projects Rule to those weeks and to account for events (which usually take a slot) and recurring projects.

If you're like most people, you'll need to take a couple of passes to revise your weekly projects, as the first pass is usually overoptimistic even when people use the Five Projects Rule. Remember that you're committing to important projects you'll finish, not everything you might work on.

Once you've started with the month-level perspective, you can decide to zoom up to larger perspectives of time pretty easily. Many people find it easier to jump to the annual perspective from there, since they can then see how the quarters roll into each other; but you probably don't need to go down any further than the monthly time perspective for future quarters, since doing so would be planning too far in advance.

Also, if you're a top-down planner, it may be easier for you to start with your five projects for the year and work down to the monthly view. The good news is that the steps are the same, but you'll just need to make some substitutions for time perspectives.

Since the 5/10/15 split is such a powerful aid in helping you keep your momentum going, give yourself a focus block to make the momentum plan for the month, following the steps above. You'll definitely find it easier to use the free Monthly Momentum Planner download available at startfinishingbook.com/resources, but you can also use a blank sheet of paper.

Next up, we'll be covering how to keep the bobbing and weaving going as you navigate the wins and setbacks that show up as you're doing your best work.

CHAPTER 8 TAKEAWAYS

▶ Momentum planning is the process of continually making and adjusting plans across all time perspectives.

▶ The seven environmental factors to make work for you are sound, smell, sunlight, clothing, clutter/organization, amount of space, and music.

▶ Batching work is the process of doing similar kinds of work in a contiguous stretch of time; stacking work is the process of doing dissimilar but compatible kinds of work in the same stretch of time.

▶ Frogs are the tasks and chunks of projects that we really don't want to do—addressing them more frequently helps keep the dread-to-work ratio lower.

▶ Rather than using what needs to be done as the foundation of your daily or weekly planning, make when it's best to do certain kinds of work the foundation.

▶ First in priority doesn't always mean first in sequence.

▶ The 5/10/15 split combines the Five Projects Rule with momentum planning for ten minutes before you start your work and fifteen minutes at the end of your day.

▶ Planning too far in advance can create frustration and resignation since the further out you plan, the more likely it is that your plan will be incorrect.

How we spend our days is,
of course, how we live our lives.
ANNIE DILLARD, *The Writing Life*

BUILD DAILY MOMENTUM

When we think about thriving, we tend to think big picture, but the reality is that it's the accumulation of purposeful and productive days that lead to our thriving. We become by doing, and the days are where the doing happens.

But the days of our lives are where distractions, interruptions, and the consequences of our decisions come home to roost. It's where we need to bob, weave, step, and dance our way to getting through the voids of the projects on deck. The good news is that we have 365 days a year to start finishing our best work; the bad news is that it's surprisingly easy for a day to get away from us and to undercount the importance of any single day.

The steps we take today create a different path for tomorrow. And since each step counts, let's start there.

CELEBRATE SMALL WINS SO YOU CAN CELEBRATE BIGGER ONES

Your best work is going to be broken into projects that often are going to require months, quarters, and years to complete. But between when you start a project and when you finish it may be a lot of daily setbacks, cascades, thrashing, and existential mini crises that, combined, are enough to make you lose track of the picture and career into a thrash crash.

It's also true that with almost every block of time you allocate to your project, you move it forward. The exceptions are when you're generally thrashing or when you're almost to the finish line, but even still, those bouts of flailing are part of the process. Staying on the field while flailing is better than checking out completely.

As much as we've focused on finishing, the more nuanced truth is that progress is what matters more. While you may finish discrete projects, you'll never be finished with your best work. Each completed project is just the start of one or more other projects, and, as you succeed and evolve, the goalposts on your best work will change. To make progress, you have to finish projects, and while that comes with a great deal of satisfaction, it's usually not the end goal.

Progress being the more important goal also allows us to accommodate our experience that the happiness that comes with completing a project is fleeting at best. It's quite common to invest the limits of our blood, sweat, and tears into a best-work project only to step back when it's done and think, "That's it?!" At a certain point, the joy is in the process and progress, not the product, but for some of us, the product of our work is the basis of our livelihood.

But if progress trumps completion, it also means that all the smaller chunks of work we finish every day are worth celebrating in their own right.

Of course, when I say celebrate, I'm not talking about throwing a party every day—though if that's how you roll, I'm not judging. What I mean is to take a moment to acknowledge that you showed up, and in the midst of an overdistracted, overpressured, and overurgent world, you finished something that mattered.

I find it odd that daily celebrations are a novel concept that I sometimes have to fight for when taken in the context of how many moments we spend ruminating on what *didn't* go the way we wanted it to. We can just steal some of our daily self-deprecation and spend it on daily celebrations. At the very least, the daily celebrations allow us to counter the negative stories we reinforce, generate, or absorb every day.

SRINIVAS RAO   DON'T BREAK THE CHAIN

When it comes to our most ambitious creative projects, we often don't celebrate them until we've poured blood, sweat, and tears into them. But it doesn't have to be that way. The simple act of tracking our progress isn't only proven to increase motivation but it also improves our sense of fulfillment when we're working on a project.

The simplest version of this was popularized by Jerry Seinfeld, when a young comedian asked him for advice on how to become a better comedian. Seinfeld told him to buy a calendar, and for every day he wrote jokes, he should mark an *X* on the calendar. Eventually there would be a chain, and the goal was simply not to break the chain.

When we're able to see our progress, we don't have to delay gratification, and progress creates motivation and momentum. Instead of letting our well-being be determined entirely by outcomes, we're able to do so with our effort. Your effort, actions, and behavior are always in your control.

Commit to a consistent action, measure your effort, and your fulfillment and motivation will go through the roof.

Srinivas Rao is the author of *An Audience of One: Reclaiming Creativity for Its Own Sake* and the host of the *Unmistakable Creative* podcast, where he's interviewed more than seven hundred people.

Here are some ways you can celebrate your small wins:

▸ **Create a win journal in which you highlight three wins every day.** They need not all be related to your best work, and if you already have something such as a gratitude journal, you can add a little section about wins. This is also part of the 5/10/15 split, but you may want to account for your wins later in the evening or before bed to capture the full day. Going to sleep having anchored your wins leads to much more restful sleep than going to bed with your setbacks or frustrations in mind.

▸ **Share small wins with other people.** It may not seem noteworthy that you finished a piece of something, but it is, and there's a good chance that your friends and success pack will take interest, be excited, and celebrate with you.

▸ **Keep a project and/or streak tracker.** It's one thing to create a streak or some momentum on a project; it's another, more powerful thing to see that you've done so reliably for the last three months. This tracker can become an amazing tool to shift stories about yourself, for it's evidence that you can do what you set your mind to.

If you don't create a practice of celebrating the small wins, it's harder to celebrate the big wins, for two reasons: (1) the small wins get you through the void so that you can create the bigger wins, and (2) if you can celebrate what may seem like insignificant wins, the more significant wins will be all the easier to acknowledge and celebrate. Something I've learned through my own work and with clients is that the practice of celebrating small wins shifts the language and mindset around the big wins—rather than "that happened," it becomes "I/we made it happen." There's less of an appeal to mystery, luck, or chance and more of an acknowledgment that it was our actions that led to the result.

And, of course, there's no mystery to that shift:

it's easy to see what led to the big win when you've been celebrating and keeping up with all the small wins along the way.

CREATE HABITS AND ROUTINES THAT MAKE IT EASIER TO BUILD AND MAINTAIN MOMENTUM

While we're on creating a habit of celebrating small wins, let's talk more generally about habits and routines. Both are examples of defaults—that is, behaviors that are automatic or don't require choosing every time. They're incredibly helpful because they lower the cognitive and energetic requirements of the day by removing scores of daily microdecisions that drain the finite amount of energy we have each day. Every choice we don't have to make lets us focus that energy on things that actually matter, and it all adds up.

The not-so-secret secret to defaults is that, given that we're creatures of habit, we naturally create defaults, but the defaults we naturally create are rarely the ones that lead to our thriving. As a general rule, naturally generated defaults tend to center on comfort, pleasure, and survival, largely because our biological wiring rewards those conditions. Our biological wiring is also such that the more frequently we do something, the more likely we are to do it the next time—as neuropsychologist Donald Hebb said, "what fires together, wires together."

So any discussion of defaults has to start with the reality that we already have some defaults, and we can create more and different defaults. The question is how to create and maintain the defaults that work for us and minimize the ones that work against us. The momentum planning method, the 5/10/15 split, and time blocking are all examples of defaults we've been building to make space for our best work, but let's take a look at habits and routines in more detail.

HABITS

Habits are single behaviors that are so ingrained that you have to inhibit doing those habits when their trigger is present. There's a way you tie your shoes, brush your teeth, or eat certain kinds of food that you would have to actively try to do differently, and you still might fail. You also have a default way that you interact with your devices; many channel flippers don't consciously choose to flip channels any more than they choose to tie their shoes certain ways.

Anchors are habits that are focused around environments and tools. Environments are the containers we do habits in, and tools are the things that trigger certain habits. The hard part of exercising for many people isn't what happens *in the gym* but in getting *to the gym.* Once you're there, it's more than just thinking you might as well do something since you're there; the environment itself makes getting your sweat on the default option that you have to decide against. It's subtler, but the same thing happens when you walk into a conference room, your office, or your parents' house.

Since we know that shifts happen with places and tools, we can choose to build our habits around those places—this is one of the reasons we took so much time in the last chapter on making sure your environment works for you. But, as with all habits, we have to actively create and cultivate anchors for them to have their power. If you want to do your best work on your kitchen table, you'll need to make sure that you *don't* continually do admin work at your kitchen table with the same tool, as it doesn't set the anchor. If you want to use your tablet for deep reading, it doesn't help if the same tablet is where you watch movies and play video games.

ROUTINES

Routines are habits or behaviors that are consistently done in the same sequence or at the same time. They're the equivalent of molecules, with habits being the individual atoms that make up the molecule. The major upshot of routines is that the only choice you need to make is to *start* the routine; the rest of the sequence has the inertia to complete itself.

Routines create flow, which is why there's such an appeal and case for morning routines, regardless of our chronotype. Larks put in their work earlier in the day and owls later in the day, but each can have an entire prework routine that looks pretty similar. Biological functions undergird so much of our routines—*when* we eat and go to the bathroom is what varies, not that we need to.

But morning routines are just one type of routine we can create. The following are some others that will lighten your cognitive load:

- **Bedtime routines.** What series of actions will best set you up for a good night of sleep? Something as simple as drinking a glass of water, brushing your teeth, laying out the next day's outfit, and writing in your gratitude or win journal may create a downcycling period that helps you ease into sleep better than trying to sleep abruptly after screen time.

- **Work warm-up routines.** What sequence of actions would best set you up for work? If you commute, consider the first five actions you do and whether there's a better arrangement. For instance, checking email and voicemail could be *last* in the sequence rather than first in the sequence. If you work from home, having a routine that clearly demarcates the different periods of your day can be incredibly helpful in avoiding a continual mashup of work, chores, distractions, and filler time.

- **Work checkout routines.** The 15 of the 5/10/15 split could be but a part of your work checkout routine. Yours may include organizing your desk, removing dishes, getting books back to their proper home, making sure all your work is saved to the cloud, and so on.

- **After-work routines.** If you commute to work, this may include consistent actions such as putting your handbag, keys, wallet, and phone in certain places, cleaning trash out of the car, and so on. But it could also include meditating, listening to music, exercising first thing, and doing other activities that put a buffer between the energy of the office and home. If you're working from home, it can be many of the same things, and you probably need *more* routines to create the buffer between modes of working. The fifteen-foot walk from the kitchen table to the couch often means that you just drag the cognitive work from the kitchen table to the couch with you.

- **Cold-start routines.** It can be hard to get back into your best work if it's been a few days since you've been in it. A cold-start routine is a list of things you do to get back in the groove. It may sound like overkill, but I printed out my cold-start routine for drafting while I was writing this book, and I would reread and follow the steps when I had missed more than three or four days writing due to my schedule and health challenges.

- **Chore routines.** Chores have to get done, but it can be really helpful to create a chore routine such that you almost automatically get them done. At the very least, it can help you avoid getting distracted and leaving the chores half done.

Given that we're creatures of habit, you probably already have some habits or behaviors that you do for each of the kinds of work or transitions listed above. You can build on those habits—what's often called *habit stacking*—to create a flow of purposeful activity that tends to things that matter, all without having to decide every time. While your body is going through the motions, your brain can focus on something else or downcycle and recover from whatever it was processing before.

For instance, using the list of routines on the previous page, you could roll from your work checkout routine to your after-work routine to your chore routine—in fact, your after-work routine may contain your chore routine—and this may create a simple flow that then opens up the rest of the evening for you to be more fully present with other stuff that matters or that allows you to be in full-on recharge mode.

LEAVE YOURSELF A CRUMB TRAIL

Consider two truths: (1) it's usually easy to tell what the next step of a project is at the end of a working session, and (2) it can be incredibly hard to figure out what the next step is at the start of a working session. Part of the reason we can get entranced with our best work is that, once we get on a roll, it's really easy to keep it up. Likewise, part of the reason we avoid our best work is that the colder the project is, the harder it is to get started.

Leaving a crumb trail is the practice of giving yourself easy ways to get back into your work. It comes from the "Hansel and Gretel" fairy tale,[1] and, in case it's

---

1. This metaphor is also used in web design to refer to the convention of displaying to the reader how they got to a particular place on a website.

been a while since you've heard it, Hansel and Gretel leave a crumb trail to avoid getting lost in the woods. The metaphor is apt, though we do need to overlook the part about the crumb trail being eaten by animals.

Leaving ourselves bread crumbs requires us to do two things we're often not particularly good at: (1) leaving ourselves enough time at the end of a focus block to leave bread crumbs and (2) forecasting that the momentum we have at the end of a focus block won't be there at the start of the next. What we more often do is use all our available time trying to finish something and then slide into something else. But that white-knuckled focus and slide make it incredibly challenging to get started the next time, so we spend a lot of time getting back into the project, only to repeat the cycle anew.

Furthermore, we often assume that we'll be able to get back into the project before it goes cold on us, but life has an annoying habit of not following the way we think it will go. It's not just that our project and planned focus blocks can get displaced, but something can happen in between the end of one planned focus block and the next one such that we get spun around and lost in the woods.

The irony is that once you assume you'll be lost at the start of the next focus block and prepare for it by leaving bread crumbs, it becomes significantly harder to be lost at the start of your next focus block. Once leaving bread crumbs becomes a habit, daily momentum becomes a reality.

Here are some ways to leave yourself bread crumbs:

▸ At the end of a work session—which may be the end of one focus block or the end of the last of back-to-back focus blocks—leave a quick note to yourself about where to pick up.

▸ If you were truly in flow and lost track of time, your fallback time to leave yourself bread crumbs is at the end of the day during the 5/10/15 split. While it's not as optimal as at the end of the working session, it's better than starting cold the next morning or at your first focus block of the day.

▸ Consider using author Ernest Hemingway's trick of stopping before you're empty and leaving something easy to start with.[2] You want it to be easy enough that it doesn't take a lot of brainpower but difficult enough that you have to engage with it.

While we've been discussing bread crumbs in the context of active projects, another helpful practice is to make sure that all on-hold or stuck projects have bread crumbs, which might be as simple as being clear about what the next action is. The bread crumbs for projects on hold might indicate the conditions needed to start the project or the reasons why it's on hold, whereas the bread crumbs for stuck projects may indicate why they're stuck. In both cases, the bread crumbs

---

2. One of Ernest Hemingway's many writing tips is: "And remember to stop while you are still going good. That keeps it moving instead of having it die whenever you go on and write yourself out. When you do that you find that the next day you are pooped and can't go on." Larry W. Phillips, ed., *Ernest Hemingway on Writing* (New York: Touchstone, 1999), 217. It applies to all creative work, not just writing novels.

keep you from having to wonder what's going on with that particular project every time you look at it.

Because bread crumbs often amount to microplans, like all plans, they don't have to be followed. As you ruminate over your work, you may have an insight, epiphany, or realization that makes it clear that something different needs to happen. You can follow that thread, and even if that trail isn't fruitful, you still have your old bread crumbs to keep you from aimlessly wandering in the creative wilderness. If the new trail is fruitful, you can evaluate if your crumb trail is still relevant or if it leads to a diversion.

MINIMIZE INTERRUPTIONS AND DISTRACTIONS

While we're on environments, it's a good time to think about the distractions and interruptions that may be keeping you from doing your best work. I lump them together because they're unplanned diversions from your work, but their causes are fundamentally different, so addressing them requires different responses.

Let's take a look at the key differences between interruptions and distractions:

▶ **Interruptions are external diversions that keep us from doing our best work.** These are things such as children walking into the room, incoming phone calls, and coworkers knocking on the door (despite the rule of not knocking if the door's closed).

▶ **Distractions are internal diversions that we allow ourselves to do.** Email, social media, YouTube, past seasons of *Battlestar Galactica*, or that new *O, The Oprah Magazine* fall into this category. None of these run into the room and tug on our shirt; we allow them to tug on us.

Though minimizing distractions and interruptions requires different solutions, the solutions themselves share the common thread in that they require finding the *entry point* first and examining how you can alter that entry point. Focusing on the entry point prevents the distraction or interruption rather than reacting to it, for once you're distracted or interrupted—especially during deep work—you've lost the thread and may not be able to recover it easily.

Take email, for instance. While it may be true that the notification settings on your devices may seem to be interruptions, you enable those notifications. If you can choose to disable them but decide not to, then you have allowed yourself to be distracted. If you change these notifications, the only way you can be diverted by email is if you *check* email; the entry points for email are thus the devices and apps that allow you to check email. If you eliminate or minimize those entry points, you make it harder to be distracted by email. We were less distracted by email fifteen years ago simply because we didn't have notification engines in our pocket and there wasn't the expectation of near-instantaneous responses.

INTERRUPTING INTERRUPTIONS

Of the two, interruptions tend to be the harder to minimize or eliminate because they (usually) involve other living beings; realizing as water drips on your head that you have a roof leak is also an interruption, but these kinds of interruptions are rarer for most of us.

For ease of explanation, I'll call being mostly uninterruptible being *dark*, understanding that most of the time you'll want to go dark for focus blocks, but you may also go dark for recovery blocks.

Going dark requires boundary conversations and negotiations, so it's useful to break these conversations down by the kinds of people you're addressing:

- **Bosses.** Because of the power dynamic, boss interruptions can be the hardest to minimize or eliminate because not being interruptible can lead to not having a job to be interrupted at. Fortunately your boss's interest and yours likely align; they want you to do more and better work, and you want to do more and better work. Thus framing your need to go dark so you can do more and better work is common ground to build from.

- **Coworkers.** Starting with your boss makes minimizing interruptions from coworkers a lot easier since your dark time is sanctioned by your boss. In most cases, negotiating commonly available times with coworkers is a welcome relief for many teams, since it dislodges the "always available" mindset that few of us actually talk about but most of us follow.

- **Adult(ish) family.** While kids and pets tend to be worse about interruptions than adult(ish) family, it's your adult(ish) family that can help you address the interruptions from kids and who also can be a huge interruption engine. By adult(ish), I include teenagers who are mostly capable of taking care of themselves, younger kids, and pets if properly motivated to do so. Going dark from adult(ish) family is largely about bartering free/dark time and ensuring you have similar conventions in place as you do with your work team about what's relevant to break your dark periods and how to contact you.

- **Children.** While rules around interrupting you while working and/or not knocking on closed doors can help with interruptions from children, following rules is something kids aren't often good at—and that's not even counting babies and toddlers. Going dark with kids amounts to two strategies: (1) having an adult(ish) family member take sole responsibility for caretaking while you're dark and (2) physically going somewhere else while that surrogate caretaking is in play. Fortunately time may be your ally here in the sense that your kids may be at school, attending after-school activities, or, in the case of younger ones, asleep during times in which you could be dark from other interruption sources.

You may need to address other people such as clients, neighbors, and friends, but those are much more contextual and murkier than the relationships above. If your friend is going through a nasty divorce, you may be on the other end of a lot of interruptions, as they need to process it with you; in most cases and with most other friends, you may not be as interruptible as you are for the in-crisis friend. Your neighbor's love for their way-too-loud motorcycle may be hell on your emu-aligned evening work session, but it may be unreasonable to expect them to not work on their bike while you're painting. Clients may hire you or your company precisely because they want someone else to be interruptible on demand, in which case they have a legitimate claim to your being (reasonably) interruptible.

Once you open the door for dark periods, you can assess what entry points to close. For work contexts, the common entry points are your (smart)phone, email (computer), collaboration hubs such as Slack (computer), and your door or area if you work in an open office. Some combination of switching environments, shutting down apps, and going on wireless mode is going to be the right dark setup for you. If you work from home, you merely replace your door or desk with analogs at home, but you add the sources mentioned above, so it still boils down to the same combinations above with making sure the kids/pets are cared for and/or kept out. Most smartphones have a Do Not Disturb mode and settings that allow you to specify recurring times and people who can get through when your phone is set to Do Not Disturb; setting this up makes sure that you can be interruptible to certain people at certain times but aren't disturbed by robocalls and others who "just want to talk."

DEALING WITH DISTRACTIONS

A chief reason we need to discuss distractions and interruptions separately is to avoid the common pattern of finding ourselves frittering away a dark period or a planned focus block with things we choose to be distracted by. It's far too easy to create the time, space, and environment we need only to fall into a click hole, email, or conversation that we didn't need to initiate or respond to.

We rarely consciously choose to be distracted, and we don't intend on being distracted for as long as we actually end up being distracted. Few people go to Facebook intending to spend forty-five minutes scrolling and arguing with strangers. One YouTube video seems to turn into seven. The quick call to your friend turns into a thirty-seven-minute replay of what her son's teacher did to him yesterday.

Digital distractions can be especially devastating to our momentum because of how easy it is to fall into what I call the "Infinite Loop of Digital Distractions" (hereafter the Loop). An email contains a link to a website; the website contains a few links, pop-ups, and share options; a share option sends you to a social media site and the thing you just had to sign up for is sitting in your inbox; somewhere along the way you were given an option to buy something or remembered that there was something you meant to pick up from Amazon, so you need to get your wallet; by the time you get back with your wallet or finish reviewing the thirteen different options for the thing on Amazon, there's a new important email that came in or you remember that you need to prep for your upcoming meeting; after the meeting or email, you now have six open tabs and need to check likes, comments, or responses on the link you shared. The entirety of our unplanned moments throughout a given day can be spent on the Loop, and if the way I've explained it sounds maddening, absurdly comical, and tedious, I've done an adequate job of capturing reality.

The problem isn't that we're distracted for a moment but that we get on the Loop where the combination of microgoal completion and dopamine keep us on it. In the moment, it seems as if we're getting somewhere, and it feels satisfying, but we're the rocking chair that's all motion and no progress. In reality, it's retrogress, for as we've been rocking, time has been tick-tocking.

Much like interrupting interruptions, the simplest way to deal with distractions is to block the distraction entry points. For example, it's impossible to get distracted by YouTube if you don't have access to a connected device. Distractions thus follow the same pattern as interruptions: the harder it is to distract yourself, the less likely you are to be distracted.

The strategies below get successively more aggressive at blocking distractions, so if distractions are displacing your best work, work your way down the list:

▸ **Make your daily momentum plan before jumping onto distraction sources.** The 5/10/15 split is particularly helpful here because you can reference the plan you made yesterday at the end of the day and thus start with a default. Even if you need to check email or your collaboration hub, you're only looking to *update* your plan rather than starting from scratch, and your default plan may have enough weight to pull you out of the Loop.

▸ **Create better defaults during transition periods to replace the distracting defaults you may have.** For instance, rather than checking email first, walk the halls at work or around the block at home. I personally leave my office after every meeting because if I don't, I'm more likely to get on the Loop and lose what might otherwise be a recovery block.

▸ **Turn off all notifications and make ample use of Do Not Disturb.** If whatever it is has a way to be silenced, do so. Turning off *all* notifications is a better starting point than eliminating one or two, with the caveats that you make sure (1) you have the conversations highlighted in the section on interruptions and (2) you have enough admin blocks to keep up with the required administrivia that comes with every job.

▸ **Lock yourself out.** Since turning off notifications may not be enough to prevent the first click of the Loop, you may need to block your ability for the first click to turn into a second. There are lots of ways to block apps and websites. I currently use and recommend Cold Turkey Blocker (for the Mac) and Screen Time (for the iPhone), but these options are always evolving as technology companies recognize that they've gotten too good at creating devices that make distraction a habit.

▸ **Delete apps or remove capabilities.** If blocking apps isn't enough to keep you out, then remove the apps completely. I routinely sit with clients while they remove distracting apps from their phones, sometimes including email and their browser. All modern computer operating systems allow you to create accounts that can only open specific apps and/or can't open specific websites, so you could log into a "Best Work" or "Creator" account that only allows you to do your best work. Turning off your Wi-Fi or removing your Wi-Fi card may also prevent you from getting on the Loop.

▸ **Use dumbtech.** It's inconvenient, but using devices that don't have internet or distracting capabilities makes distraction (from those sources) impossible. For instance, many people need music to get in the zone, which they assume means that they need their smartphones, but old-school iPods play music just as well and can be found cheaply on the internet and at pawn shops. Longhand may be more inefficient than typing, but if you actually draft more and better words because you're less distracted, spending a couple of hours a week transcribing your longhand may be more effective.[3]

Finding the right combination of distraction-blocking strategies may take a little time and money, but consider how much of your week you're on the Loop, recovering from being distracted, or frustrated that the open time you had during the day was lost.

Eliminating distractions alone can generate the recommended three focus blocks per week needed to fuel a best-work project.

Since we choose to be distracted, we can choose not to be. Zooming up, if we choose to be distracted, we're also choosing to *not do* our best work. Your move.

---

3. I've written most of this book on an AlphaSmart Neo2, a digital keyboard from the late nineties that can be found on eBay for twenty-five dollars, since I draft faster and produce better work via the Neo and don't get distracted. I have to spend ten minutes every few days transferring my writing to my computer, but it's easy to spend an hour a day on the Loop or running through my action list only to find that I haven't done my drafting for the day.

CASCADES, TARPITS, AND LOGJAMS: THREE WAYS PROJECTS GET STUCK

In an ideal world, we'd build a perfect road map, our schedules would actually be what we'd planned they'd be, and there wouldn't be any disruptions to throw us off. In this world, projects get off track, and the more a project gets off track, the more likely it is to end up stuck. Just as a project in motion tends to stay in motion, a project at rest tends to stay at rest.

But projects slip and end up stuck for different reasons; knowing this helps you prevent them from getting stuck and dislodge them when they're stuck. Let's cover some of the common pitfalls that can interrupt our momentum, which I call *cascades*, *logjams*, and *tarpits*.

CASCADES

A cascade is the pattern by which one project gets behind and causes other projects to get behind. While it's sometimes true that the cascade starts because the projects are linked, projects don't have to be logically linked to start a cascade. It could simply be that the focus blocks you had planned disappear or get reallocated, so every other project that pulls against downstream focus blocks slide backward in time. Those chunks of projects start backing up on each other like a conveyer belt that has a blockage on the end. (Think of the *I Love Lucy* chocolate factory episode.)

To deal with a cascade, you have to work on both ends of the conveyor belt. If projects and commitments keep coming in at the same rate, even if you work on the end, you'll still have a backup. If you just work on the end, you'll still have a backup.

Here's how to handle a cascade:

- **Put all optional projects on hold.** An "optional" project is one that won't get you in hot water if it's not done.

- **Say no to new projects when you can.** If you keep getting more projects faster than you can do the ones you've already got on deck, you may need to show the project delegators what you have on deck and make a case for why you need a "new project timeout" for a few weeks to get caught up.

- **Sort the remaining projects by importance.** This often means prioritizing projects you're going to get in more trouble for or be embarrassed by if undone. If projects tie for importance, work on the one that can be finished first and use the snowball method until you get caught up.

- **Work on projects sequentially rather than trying to push seven at once.** Better to finish a project or two a week and use the snowball method to get caught up than to make a little progress on a handful of projects, especially if you had to negotiate for a "new project timeout" with people.

- **Use the Five Projects Rule so you can see the cascade coming.** Cascades often occur because we commit to too many projects in the first place.

You don't get out of a cascade by continuing to shuffle projects or by simply working faster; you get out of them by finishing the essential projects and committing to fewer projects once you're out of the cascade.

LOGJAMS

Logjams occur when you have too many parallel projects happening at once and you can't finish them all when you need to. Much like cascades, the project chunks don't have to be a part of the same larger project; you can simply have two large projects with simultaneous deadlines competing for the same limited focus blocks.

Here's how to clear out a logjam:

▸ **Review the conflicting projects to determine which chunks of the projects will get a project moving.** If one project starts to move, it tends to open up space for the others to move as well.

▸ **Triage your projects and renegotiate deadlines (if possible).** This means you don't have so many projects coming due at the same time.

▸ **Anticipate and address logjams before they happen.** As you're working through your project list, be on the lookout for the chunks of projects that are likely to cause snags and prioritize finishing them, so your logjam doesn't turn into a cascade.

TARPITS

A tarpit is the pattern wherein a project not only gets stuck, but the longer it stays stuck, the harder it is to pick it up again. It's the difference between throwing a ball on concrete and throwing it into a tarpit. If you've ever tried to pick up a project that's been stuck for longer than a year, you've likely experienced the "Ugh!" of a tarpit.

Here's how to handle a project stuck in a tarpit:

1 **Make sure the project isn't dead.** If it's dead, then let it go.

2 **If it's alive but just stuck, reconnect with the pain of not doing the project, with the caveat that not living up to your ideals can be a pain.** The project is stuck in the tarpit because not doing other projects feels like it would cause more pain. Rather than try to compare "it would be good to have this outcome" to "it will be painful to not have this outcome," it's usually easier to compare pain to pain.

3 **If you haven't done so, chunk the project into smaller pieces.** Because it's in the tarpit, it's usually helpful to chunk down smaller than you normally would.

4 **Pick a chunk that you can do within the next three days.** The goal here is to get *some* movement, since a project in motion is easier to keep in motion.

5 **Work on a chunk of the project at least twice a week.** This will prevent the project from sliding back into the tarpit.

6 **Avoid putting the project into a (metaphorical or literal) closet.** If you can't see the project, it's too easy for it to sink back into the tarpit. Make it so that it's easier to work on the project than to shuffle it around.

If you're continually finding that you have projects in tarpits, it's a good sign that you're overcommitted and/or committing to projects that aren't aligned with your priorities. It's probably time to go on a project diet by removing one project slot from the Five Projects Rule and continue to drop down until you start finishing 80 percent or so of the projects you commit to in the time you commit to them.

HOW TO GET THROUGH THE CREATIVE RED ZONE

Pushing a project over the finish line is often one of the hardest parts of finishing a project. It sometimes feels as if no matter how much you work on it, you have just as much to do as you did before you started the last push. I call this last stretch the *red zone* of a project because it's similar to the phenomenon we see in (American) football, where the offense gets to the last twenty yards before the end zone, only to lose the ball or, at best, have to go for a field goal rather than a touchdown.

In football, it's fairly obvious why there are so many red-zone turnovers. For one thing, the defense locks down and has less field to cover, so the offense has fewer options for how to push the ball forward. Then there's the fact that offensive players do one of three things: (1) they take it for granted that they're done and don't give their full effort, (2) they succumb to the fatigue of having driven the ball eighty yards, or (3) they get overexcited and make mistakes because they're thinking about it too much.

Creative projects have very similar patterns. The defense is the head trash, competing priorities, and poor team alignment. Whereas the dragons that keep you from creating generally have plenty of avenues to keep you from finishing and showing your work, they now can concentrate their powers in the same way that the defense in football can. And we're often tired or exasperated toward the end of a project, so we fall into overthinking or succumb to the creative fatigue that's a natural byproduct of expending so much of the mental, emotional, and physical energy needed to carry the creative ball that far. (Ironically, decision fatigue makes it more likely that we'll overthink things precisely because we don't have the inner resources to make decisions in the face of uncertainty.)

This reminds me of one of my favorite quotes from the Tao Te Ching:

People, in handling affairs,
Often come close to completion and fail
If they are as careful in the end as the beginning
Then they would have no failure.[4]

Getting through the red zone is tough. While there are a few outliers who get more positively excited toward the end of a project, most of us don't. That's why we hold on to things and stop finishing.

But you don't have to lose the ball in the red zone. Here are some things you can do to get your projects wrapped up when resistance is holding those last few yards.

DOUBLE DOWN BY RETURNING TO THE WHY OF THE PROJECT

When we shift to the hows and whens of a project, it's easy to lose sight of why we started in the first place. If nothing else, think of the beneficiaries in your success pack who will be better off when you finish and show your work. The world is a little better because of what you've been doing.

And then there's the reality that you'll be better off in the long run. You'll have one more thing that matters done, and you can be proud of what you've created. Finishing your best work is one of the greatest gifts you can give yourself.

---

4. Derek Lin, trans., *Tao Te Ching: Annotated and Explained* (Woodstock, VT: SkyLight Paths, 2006), 129.

FOCUS ON GETTING IT TO GOOD ENOUGH

As Voltaire said, "Perfection is the enemy of good," for no other reason than that perfection is unattainable, which means that if that's your goal, you'll never be done. The key to being useful and prolific is understanding that getting something to good enough is the best we can do—we need other people to make our work excellent.

KNOW THAT THE MORE IT MATTERS, THE MORE IT'S ONLY A START ANYWAY

The more the project matters to you or the people who benefit from it, the more it's only a start.

A book is only a conversation starter.

A community project is only the start of building a thriving community.

A beta application starts a relationship of delight and utility with its users.

A new diet is only the start of the lifestyle changes to create a healthier you.

A leadership initiative is just the start of greater things to come for your team.

We often falsely assume that the more it matters, the better the start should be. The reality is much humbler and accessible:

**the more something matters,
the better it is that we start finishing *sooner*.**

UNDERSTAND THAT TOWARD THE END, YOU'RE USUALLY WORKING ON YOUR OWN MINDSET

We often think that we're making the project better, yet we often have no yardstick for measuring how it's better.

An essential characteristic of the red zone is that we're continuing to work but we're not really getting anywhere;

working on it more, then, isn't going to get you any further. It just means you're going to log more hours.

What you're really working on is your own mindset. You're telling yourself that if you put more work into it, the naysayers and critics won't be able to complain about the value of your work because you gave it everything. You're telling yourself that the next addition is going to pull things together and complete the set. Or that this word, line of code, additional white space or flair, or piece of supporting research will make it that much better.

But imagine flipping this mindset to that of serving others by finishing your work. Every day you delay is a day your success pack can't help you make a bigger difference with your work.

DO YOUR WORK, THEN STEP AWAY

As Krishna told Arjuna in the Bhagavad Gita, "You have a right to your actions, but never to your actions' fruits."[5] When you do your best work, you give up the certainty of outcomes for the certainty of purpose.

5. Stephen Mitchell, trans., *Bhagavad Gita: A New Translation* (New York: Harmony, 2002), 20.

Of course, you might fail, but the silver lining is that you'll no longer be perennially stuck in the red zone. You'll get to try something with the knowledge that the last thing didn't work, so you can invest more of your energy into alternative options. Or perhaps returning to the heart of the matter will reveal that it wasn't something you should have been doing in the first place.

Better to know that today than three weeks, months, or years from now.

Again referencing Lao Tzu: "Do your work, then step back." But *step back* doesn't mean to stop working or jump right into the next thing. Step back and celebrate the journey you've been through, the dragons you've overcome, and the person you've become by doing your best work.

You've worked hard to cross that finish line and should be proud. The next chapter is about what to do once you cross it.

CHAPTER 9 TAKEAWAYS

▸ Celebrating the small wins of progress enables us to celebrate big finishes.

▸ Habits and routines minimize decision fatigue and create longer periods of flow.

▸ Leaving crumb trails for projects makes getting back into projects more enjoyable and efficient.

▸ Interruptions are external diversions that keep us from doing our best work; distractions are internal diversions that we allow ourselves to do.

▸ A project cascade happens when a project falling behind makes others fall behind; a project logjam happens when you have too many concurrent projects; and a tarpit happens when a stuck project gets more stuck the longer it stays stuck.

▸ The creative red zone is the last stretch of the project where the closer you get to the finish line, the harder it is to cross the finish line.

Great is the art of beginning,
but greater is the art of ending.

HENRY WADSWORTH LONGFELLOW,
"Elegiac Verse"

FINISH STRONG

The feeling of crossing the finish line on your best work is an exhilarating rush of ecstasy, relief, surprise, and pride. You have to lose yourself in the project only to find you're a different person on the other side, for as we create, we're creating ourselves.

Rather than just jumping to the next thing, it's time to bask in the success you've created.

RUN A VICTORY LAP

Near the end of our convoy missions, we'd cross out of Iraq and back into Kuwait. About twenty minutes after crossing the border, there was a collective, palpable sense of relief, pride, and gratitude among our soldiers. Jokes would start, inane radio chatter would need to be squelched, and parts you didn't know could clench would loosen up. We weren't done, but we at least could do it by the numbers. It was then that I knew that I wouldn't be writing any letters to family members or be a chew toy for the brass back at base.

One of the reasons I remember that feeling so vividly is that we actually had some transition time between the constant threat of ambush or mishap and being back at base, which, as a line leader, sometimes felt like a different kind of ambush zone. As a team, we had enough time to celebrate together in the ways that soldiers do—in short, we had time for a team victory lap before the busywork of base consumed our time and attention.

Victory laps are a regular feature of sports and other high-pressure events, but many of us don't realize how analogs show up elsewhere in our lives. Wedding receptions, showing new babies to friends, graduation walks, and taking friends on rides in the new car are all versions of victory laps. When we make or achieve something significant, we want to show it. But just as important, we want to be seen for making or achieving it.

Yet when it comes to our best work, we often feel differently. It seems braggy, self-centered, or juvenile to celebrate the completion of our *one* project when our heroes have done so much more and better work.

That the outcomes of our best work are unlikely to be as clear-cut as other types of work also make it hard to run a victory lap. In my story above, it was clear what success looked like: we delivered whatever we were ordered to, on time, and every soldier that we left with came back with us unharmed. We either accomplished the objectives or we didn't. It's the same with most of the other examples above.

But it always feels as if we could do more or do better than we did with our best-work projects. Given our negativity biases, even when we do share that we've finished something, we need to make sure to tell people how it could have been better or what it's missing. If we meet our goals, we comment that we didn't do a good job of setting the right goals. Rather than running the victory lap, we add a few more missed rungs to the Jacob's ladder we're adept at building.

Chapter 4 focused on setting goals from the start to help compensate for the tendency to have postcommencement goal creep. But the other important piece is sharing that original goal with your success pack, for when it's time to run your victory lap, they can rightly nudge you to celebrate and witness your victory. Sometimes the most important job of your success pack isn't to help you get to the finish line but rather to help you reflect on and amplify your successful finish.

What we so often forget, though, is that the victory lap isn't just about the victor but also the community.

Your success pack has been on the field or on the sidelines with you. Families and friends have missed you and pitched in for you in different ways. Your community has supported you and cheered you on the whole time. It's likely that someone has been inspired by what you're doing, and they're making your victory an example of what they can do. *Not* running your victory lap deprives your community of the chance to celebrate the victory they've been instrumental in accomplishing.

I've made the case for the victory lap so strong here because many people dismiss it as optional. It's no more optional than saying thank you or showing your appreciation for the big and small ways people have shown up for you. It deserves to be on your postfinish checklist just as much as anything else does.

Here are some ideas for how to run your victory lap:

▸ **Let your success pack know when you've finished your project.** It doesn't need to be elaborate or long—it can be a text that reads "Done!"—but they need to know, especially as they may have rallied to help you get through the red zone.

▸ **When appropriate, make it a staple response to "What's going on?" or "How's it been?"** Sure, the cashier at the grocery store may not want to be engaged, but coworkers, neighbors, friends, and family probably do. The barista that's made coffee for you and seen you typing away during your lunch break for six months might also be excited to know that they've been a part of the project too. Per the usual, it's probably wise to avoid mentioning it to naysayers, and be cautious with derailers who may kneecap you.

▸ **Create a milestone moment.** It might be a celebration dinner with your family. It could be a vacation, if your means allow for it. It could be a concert or a community party. As a general rule, the more intangible your best work is, the more likely that you're going to need to make it tangible and visible; the physicality of new spaces, stuff in the world, or performances often prompt the reflection in ways that intangible work doesn't.[1]

Whatever your victory lap looks like, make sure to run it. You and the people around you deserve it.

---

1. Chip and Dan Heath's *The Power of Moments: How Certain Experiences Have Extraordinary Impact* (New York: Simon and Schuster, 2017) is a great read for creating milestone moments.

MAKE SPACE AND TIME TO
TRANSITION BETWEEN PROJECTS

There's a natural tendency to want to start the next project right after finishing a major project, or at least plan that that's what you're going to do. Doing that, though, is akin to finishing a marathon only to immediately start running another. We'd understand the wear, tear, and likelihood of injury for the marathon runner, and, as you might guess, there are analogous conditions awaiting those who don't allow for recovery and transition time with their work.

There's also a corollary that follows the insight that the more it matters to you, the more you'll thrash:

the more it matters to you, the greater the need for downtime and transition time after finishing your project.

There's a lot of your heart, blood, soul, and time tied up in the project, and finishing the project releases all that energy into the world. But, importantly, that energy is released *from you*, meaning there's an energetic void in you where the project once lived. Living with that void can be unsettling, disorienting, uplifting, relieving, and anticlimactic all at the same time.

Pushing a project through the red zone also often requires a lot of discipline, boundaries, and courage, so there's residue all around you. Chores and administrivia may have piled up. Loved ones and friends may have directly supported your project or have dealt with being disconnected from you while you were plugged into the project. There may be a backlog of small projects that have accrued as you triaged your best-work project. And you may be flat-out spent after leaving it all on the field with your project—it's not at all uncommon for people to get sick right after a big finish, as if their body was holding everything together just long enough to finish.

You may be dealing with all the elements above, or it may only be one that's particularly weighty for you. In any event, it's better to plan that you'll need downtime and transition time and actually allow yourself to take it rather than assume that you'll be on point immediately following the completion of your project.

Here are some questions to help give some defaults for your transition time:

▸ What low-energy projects or tasks would either feel good to work through or relieve unnecessary pressure?

▸ Who are the people you would either like to catch up with or who would make you feel less pressure to catch up with?

▸ Do you have outlets, hobbies, or other activities that you would like to catch up on? For example, if you've been on a writing project but like gardening, catching up on your gardening would create some space without your sitting around twitching and looking for something to do.

If nothing else, you'll have some cleanup work to do after you cross the finish line, so let's discuss what that looks like.

GIVE YOURSELF TIME TO DO SOME CAT WORK— CLEAN UP, ARCHIVE, AND TRASH

The process of getting projects done is messy. Through the process, we hoard, scatter, cram, stack, lose, break, and wear out physical, mental, and digital stuff all over the place. Even when we create or maintain habits and routines that help us clean up as we go, there still tends to be a level of detritus and mess that routine sweeps miss.

After you complete a project is the perfect time for CAT (clean up, archive, and trash) work. You'll be doing this work across at least three different areas—environmental, digital, and social—but you may also need to do some CAT work in other dimensions of your life. You may also be able to clean up and trash stuff, and then archive if you're able to make quick decisions; or skip the cleanup if your routines have done a decent job of keeping things relatively organized.

Let's walk through this step by step, assuming you need to do some cleanup before making decisions about what to trash and what to archive.

CLEAN UP

Depending on how messy you've been and how much was missed during any routines you have, this could be a quick process that moves on to archive or trash, but the main point of this phase is to make sense of what's around you.

Use the list below to scan the three major areas of your life:

▸ **Environmental.** Your work environment may be your office, your kitchen table, your workshop, or wherever else you've been making stuff. Depending on what you've created, you may need to do some cleanup and maintenance on the tools you've used. Included in this cleanup and maintenance phase is restocking or replacing items that were expended throughout the process.

▸ **Digital.** Now's a good time to make sense of all the links, working files, stuff dropped on your desktop, and notes and tasks you made for yourself. It's unlikely that you're going to be able to make sense of the digital mess you've made six months from now, so if you don't do it now, it's going to hang around and clutter up your systems and brain until you've had enough and have to clean it out. I recommend backing up your device before cleaning it out, so even if you mistakenly archive or trash something, you can still get to it later.

▸ **Social.** It may be strange to put your social life as a dimension for cleanup, but it's useful to consider what needs to happen with the people around you. You may have put off a conversation while you were in the red zone and now it's time to pick it up. You may have been less-than-your-best self when you were interrupted, or committed to a follow-up or made a promise that you need to see through. You likely have a long list of thank-yous to say, as well, and don't want to get into the awkward zone where it feels too late to say it, but it also feels weird to not say it. (I'm not going to detail the archive and trash steps for the social dimension, but you may need some space (archive) or a breakup (trash) that's beyond the scope of this book.)

ARCHIVE

Once you can make sense of your creative mess, you can make good decisions about what's worth keeping and what's not. In this step we're going beyond just keeping stuff; we're going to organize things to make them easy to find when we need them in the future. No more running around the house trying to find a book or having to look at seven versions of a file to figure out which one is the most recent.

Here's how to work through what needs to be archived:

▶ **Environmental.** Archiving stuff in your environment can be as simple as putting it back where it's supposed to be, but it may also include reorganizing your environment or storing some stuff that's not being used. If you've printed out a lot of stuff, you may need to scan it or put it in labeled folders so you can retrieve it more easily later.

▶ **Digital.** In a similar vein, the archive step here centers on organizing your digital stuff so that it's out of the way and easier to retrieve later. A chief difference is our natural tendency to keep a lot of duplicate files or slightly different versions. It seems like a good idea at the time but later creates more work as we try to figure out which file is the right one, or we have to check every item in a search. Even if you want to keep all the different versions, naming the final file "FINAL" makes it easier to spot in the future. A little bit of archiving now goes a long way later.

TRASH

Since you've cleaned up or archived everything else that matters, you can get rid of what doesn't. "Trashing" could mean recycling, donating, or throwing something away. The main point is that it's something *you* no longer need, so there's no point in hanging on to it, and the sooner it's gone, the better. The longer you hold on to it, the harder it's going to be to get rid of in the future.

Here's how to work through what needs to be trashed:

▸ **Environmental.** Physical stuff is harder to get rid of but generally easier to reacquire if you need it. The obvious exceptions to this are unique items such as heirlooms, high-end equipment, and so on, but those items typically aren't the ones that are going to get in the way of the next project.

▸ **Digital.** Since you have a backup of the mess, deleting files is much easier. If you make a mistake, you can always retrieve it from your backup. Unless you produce or edit audio, video, or high-resolution images, it's unlikely that you'll take up enough space to be an issue.

I'm very aware that CAT work may sound slightly more appealing than dental work—it's a frog that many of us, myself included, would rather not do.

But, like all frogs, it's not a matter of if you'll need to do some CAT work but how bad it will be when you have to do it.

Not doing it during your project transition time means that you'll inevitably have to do it at the most inconvenient time during another project.

The printer will run out of toner right before you need to print off something to show to someone else. Or someone will ask for a file while you're on a trip and you'll have to spend an afternoon trying to find the right file. Or you'll spill coffee on the stack in the corner of your desk or kitchen table right as you're headed for your commute or off to an important meeting and thus have to choose between saving the stack or being late (again).

So, since you're intentionally between projects (right?), still close enough to the project for your mess to be intelligible, and needing some low-energy work to do, there's no better time to do the CAT work that's going to make your future work that much easier to do. I'll take it one step further: CAT work is actually *part* of the project and thus a part of fully finishing it.

AFTER-ACTION REVIEWS MAKE YOUR NEXT PROJECT EASIER, BETTER, AND MORE FUN

Throughout the stages of getting the project done, you've had a lot of wins as well as varying degrees of setbacks and challenges, and you've figured out how to get and keep momentum. Many of those elements will be common across other projects, and much like using your GATES, you can start your next project leveraging those lessons learned rather than learning them all over again. Learning something once is an investment; learning it twice is a waste.

After nearly every Army training activity, exercise, or event, an after-action review (AAR) is conducted, wherein participants from the event review it to improve operational efficiency, enhance training, and convert the experience into institutional memory. In most cases, the AAR is part of a checklist such that the event isn't done until an AAR is completed. They're so ubiquitous that soldiers often joke about needing to do them for the most minor and banal activities such as sweeping the floor or doing one push-up.

But more important than the efficiency, training, and shared-memory elements mentioned above is that it instills

Think about your allies and social support network. Which had the greatest influence on you—when they showed up to help during times of trouble (picking you up at 3:00 a.m. after that flat tire, being available when you got a poor prognosis from the doctor) or when things went right (celebrating your promotion or your personal record in the gym)?

We've been culturally trained to believe that a good friend is there when life is difficult. In the last ten years, science has flipped the script to show that being supportive when others disclose triumphs and joys is the better predictor of relationship satisfaction, intimacy, commitment, and stability. This seems silly—why does anyone need your enthusiastic interest and questions that augment the details, prolonging their happiness? After all, they had the positive event, not you.

The reason is that support for positive disclosures is a safe way to test the alarm of whether someone truly cares about your welfare. What can you do with this knowledge?

▸ You possess a new lens for discerning which friends to invest in (or with great pain, trim).

▸ With deliberate practice of being there when things go right, you can disrupt habits and scripts to develop and sustain healthier, satisfying relationships.

▸ You can be empowered to shape the relationships that are most desirable for your life. Instead of being a pawn who is passive, reactive, with little sense of control, you can be an originator who is active, responsible, with a profound sense of agency.

A world-recognized authority on well-being, strengths, social relationships, stress, and anxiety, Dr. Todd Kashdan, professor of psychology at George Mason University, has published over two hundred scholarly articles and is the author of *The Upside of Your Dark Side: Why Being Your Whole Self—Not Just Your "Good" Self—Drives Success and Fulfillment*, among other books.

in everyone a habit of continuous improvement, at all levels. Though soldiers may joke about doing an AAR after sweeping the floors, the thought process actually leads to improvements in floor sweeping and beyond.

Doing an AAR for your projects can have the same effect.

Rather than just mentally working through the questions below, I recommend writing down your answers in bullet form. That way, when it's time to do your next project, you can review your last AAR rather than rely on your memory to do so. Our faulty memories, when they do work, are far more likely to recall setbacks and challenges than the wins and practices that led to our success.

The following are questions to ask during your AAR. The goal is to be as honest as you can with your answers—this isn't the time to sugarcoat things or pile on yourself.

1 **What went well?** This question is fairly straightforward, and we're starting with it even though the natural tendency is to anchor on the next question. This question need not be focused merely on outcomes: consider the people, processes, and tools that made the project go well.

2 **What setbacks, challenges, or missteps did I experience?** This question is also straightforward. Don't forget to include challenges you had with other people or your planning, environment, or tools.

3 **What did I learn?** This question is intentionally broad to cover project-specific lessons as well as those that are evergreen. Did you discover that you had a particular strength or weakness that you discounted? Did you learn a new key skill or gain insight into how key players in your ecosystem interact?

4 What habits, practices, or routines do I want to keep doing going forward? To get through the void and red zone of your last projects, you likely had to develop or reinforce some habits, practices, or routines. For instance, I learned very early on while writing this manuscript that trying to draft from home wasn't working, so I started going to a coffee shop that's about three quarters of a mile from my house. As much as I'd rather write from home (in theory), in practice, going to the coffee shop is a routine that I'll likely keep doing when it's time to get some drafting done.

5 Were there any especially important difference-makers to the project? For this question, consider difference-makers that go both ways. Your answer can repeat or elevate items already listed, as this question is the one that captures the top items you'll want to remember in the future. For instance, a major difference-maker for this project was the health issue that ate up four months of the time I had to finish the book. But another (positive) difference-maker was retroactively creating a per diem budget and checking account for myself to allow myself to sink into the flow of working from the aforementioned coffee shop.

As you can see from some of the items I highlighted from my experience, what gets captured will vary from significant (four months of pain and discomfort eating up my writing time) to what may seem to be minor (going to a coffee shop to write). But capturing them all and reviewing them at the start of your next major project is incredibly helpful. For instance, if I happen to be lamenting or overwhelmed by how big a book project feels, remembering that I still completed this one on time despite losing four months will help me see that I'll likely be able to do the next one on the timeline I agree to. And I know to plan on going to the coffee shop and bake that into my plans and budgets unless I've created a better environment.

Your first few project AARs may create significant changes in the way you do your next projects. As you continue to do them, you may find that you "only" improve 1 to 5 percent per project. But 1 to 5 percent per project over a decade of projects amounts to astonishing improvements in your effectiveness, efficiency, and momentum. A focus block at the start of your project (to review previous and other relevant AARs) and at the end (to create a new one) is a small price to pay for what you'll get out of the process.

YOU HAVE UNLOCKED NEW POSSIBILITIES BY FINISHING YOUR PROJECT

Along the way of completing your best work, you've overcome dragons, handled a horde of frogs, assembled a team, navigated a few logjams and tarpits, negotiated with derailers, shaped time, and tussled with your inner demons. You've been on quite the quest.

But you've also unlocked new realities, opportunities, and mastery by completing your project. And while "new realities" may seem to be out there, it's actually true: there are conditions in this world that wouldn't exist had you not done it when, how, and with whom you did it.

Every best-work project you finish leaves more of your fingerprints on the universe.

If nothing else, completing your project has spawned more projects. The nature of our best work is that we're never done, and many of us create work and projects that carry on even after our death. The finish of one project is just the start of many others.

While it's not an exhaustive list, the completion of your project may have unlocked new:

Projects. Is there a new idea or project that can claim the place in your five projects that this one just opened up?

GATES. What GATES did you cultivate, or what new ones got added to your array?

Communities. What new communities did you work your way into?

Mindsets and stories. What self-defeating story has your victory made untrue or what positive story has your victory made true?

Portfolio points. Did you complete a project you need to show the world on your portfolio, resume, or vita?

You may be in a position where someone is responsible for giving you feedback on your work and career progression, but even in those scenarios, you're responsible for writing and updating the story of your work and career. You're doing the work to make the story, so go ahead and do the work of writing the story.

As important and powerful as finishing is, it's important that we put it in the proper context. The following Buddhist aphorism captures the tension nicely:

Before enlightenment: chop wood, carry water.
After enlightenment: chop wood, carry water.

We often believe that after we complete a significant project or journey, our life will be fundamentally different, but we often find that our life pretty much looks the same. If we place too much attachment on the world being different and better, it inevitably leads to frustration and suffering. But there's also another insight embedded in the aphorism: after we accomplish something significant, we need to return to doing what we did to get there. Understanding the aphorism from a place of expected outcomes misses that it's also about process and practice.

So, yes, set goals, make plans, put the plans to work, and navigate the void to go from idea to done. Celebrate the victories you accrue and be proud of the work. But when your work is done, take a breather, set new sights, and start finishing anew.

Before success, start finishing.

After success, start finishing.

When it comes to your best work, that's both all there is to it and all there can ever be. Days spent doing your best work compound to create a thriving life.

Start finishing today.

CHAPTER 10 TAKEAWAYS

▸ A victory lap is a social activity that you and your supporters need.

▸ The more a project matters to you, the greater the need for downtime and transition time after finishing it.

▸ Giving yourself CAT (clean up, archive, and trash) time will make the next project easier to do because you won't be fighting the messes of your last project.

▸ After-action reviews make every project a learning experience at the same time that they set you up for greater success in future projects.

▸ Finishing a best-work project unlocks new realities.

ACKNOWLEDGMENTS

It takes a village to raise children and, it turns out, to write books. I'm grateful and humbled at how big the village behind and within this book is. This is *our* book as much as it is *my* book.

Thank you to my amazing agent, David Fugate, for believing in me and this book, editing the proposal so that it sang, and navigating a brilliant pathway to get this book placed with the right publisher. Thank you to the entire Sounds True team, but especially Haven Iverson, for being the perfect editorial partner for the book, and Kira Roark, for joining conversations about the book a year early so we could bake marketing ideas into the book itself. And thanks to Todd Sattersten, whose editorial and strategic partnership has been invaluable at every step along the way. Without David, Haven, Kira, and Todd, this book would not exist.

Thank you to Jonathan Fields, Susan Piver, Pamela Slim, Cory Huff, Karen Wright, Noah Brochman, and Jeffrey Davis for being my chosen siblings and mastermind buddies whose feedback, patient ears, encouragement, counsel, and belief helped me overcome the drag points and celebrate the wins along the way. Thanks for being with me when it was my turn to ride the book publishing bull; let's keep this rodeo going, y'all.

Thank you to my amazing Productive Flourishing team, past and present: Shannon McDonough, Josephine Fannin, Jess Sommers, Catherine Oliver, Ashley Zuberi, Dusti Arab, Emma Hand, Marissa Bracke, Sarah Marie Lacy, Lisa Wood, and Michelle Mangen. This book is the byproduct of years of work that each of you have contributed to or supported in your own unique ways.

Thank you Seth Godin, Pamela Slim, Jonathan Fields, Mike Vardy, James Clear, Srinivas Rao, Chelsea Dinsmore, Susan Piver, Marc and Angel Chernoff, Jeffrey Davis,

Todd Kashdan, Jacquette Timmons, Joshua Becker, Jeff Goins, and Ishita Gupta for adding your voices to this book. Your work nourishes so many people—myself included—and I'm excited to be able to shine more light on your work.

Thank you to Vanessa Van Edwards, Emiliya Zhivotovskaya, Cynthia Morris, Jonathan Mead, David Moldawer, Tara Gentile, Joel Zavlosky, Mike Ambassador Bruny, Jamie Teasdale, Terry St. Marie, Clay Hebert, Tim Grahl, Larry Robertson, Jen Hoffman, Lisa Buyer, Leo Babauta, Josh Kaufman, Niki Papadopoulos, Chris Brogan, Willie Jackson, Naomi Dunford, Jennifer Louden, JD Roth, Johnny B. Truant, Jenny Blake, Mark Silver, Yvonne Ator, Michael Bungay Stanier, Ali Luke, Luna Jaffe, and Jenn Labin for the support, inspiration, feedback, and ideas throughout the years. Each of you has touched me and this book in ways that you may not realize.

Thank you to the Productive Flourishing community members, who have been reading, showing up to calls, sharing your stories, giving feedback, and sharing my work with your communities. Your encouragement, questions, nudges, stories, and patronage fuel me and my work; it's been over a decade and we're *still* just getting warmed up. Keep standing tall and doing your best work.

Thank you to my family—the Gilkeys, Wheelers, Ruths, Brownmillers, and Swearingens—who have always encouraged me to dream bigger and supported me, even though my journey has taken me far from home. I am who I am because you are who you are.

My wife, Angela Wheeler, is the hardest person to adequately acknowledge but the one who deserves the most thanks. You have been a driving and catalytic force in everything I've done for the last two decades, and this book is no exception. Thank you for the meals, cat duty, last-minute proofreads, strategic soundboarding, space, financial gymnastics, coaching, and emotional support that it's taken to push this book to done. ILYB&WB.

FURTHER READING

CHAPTER 1 "SOMEDAY" CAN BE TODAY

Fields, Jonathan. *How to Live a Good Life: Soulful Stories, Surprising Science, and Practical Wisdom*. Carlsbad, CA: Hay House, 2018.

Frankl, Viktor. *Man's Search for Meaning*. Boston: Beacon Press, 2006.

Robertson, Larry. *The Language of Man: Learning to Speak Creativity*. Arlington, VA: Daymark Press, 2016.

Vanderkam, Laura. *I Know How She Does It: How Successful Women Make the Most of Their Time*. New York: Portfolio, 2017.

CHAPTER 2 GETTING TO YOUR BEST WORK

Chernoff, Marc, and Angel Chernoff. *Getting Back to Happy: Change Your Thoughts, Change Your Reality, and Turn Your Trials into Triumphs*. New York: TarcherPerigee, 2018.

Hendricks, Gay. *The Big Leap: Conquer Your Hidden Fear and Take Life to the Next Level*. San Francisco: HarperOne, 2010.

Kaplan Thaler, Linda, and Robin Koval. *Grit to Great: How Perseverance, Passion, and Pluck Take You from Ordinary to Extraordinary*. New York: Currency, 2015.

Palmer, Amanda. *The Art of Asking: How I Learned to Stop Worrying and Let People Help*. New York: Grand Central, 2015.

Strecher, Victor J. *Life on Purpose: How Living for What Matters Most Changes Everything*. San Francisco: HarperOne, 2016.

CHAPTER 3 PICK AN IDEA THAT MATTERS TO YOU

Ferriss, Tim. *Tools of Titans: The Tactics, Routines, and Habits of Billionaires, Icons, and World-Class Performers*. New York: Houghton Mifflin Harcourt, 2016.

Gilbert, Elizabeth. *Big Magic: Creative Living Beyond Fear*. New York: Riverhead, 2016.

Godin, Seth. *The Dip: A Little Book That Teaches You When to Quit (and When to Stick)*. New York: Portfolio, 2007.

Goins, Jeff. *The Art of Work: A Proven Path to Discovering What You Were Meant to Do*. New York: HarperCollins Leadership, 2015.

Piver, Susan. *The Wisdom of a Broken Heart: How to Turn the Pain of a Breakup into Healing, Insight, and New Love*. New York: Atria, 2010.

Sanders, Tim. *Love Is the Killer App: How to Win Business and Influence Friends*. New York: Crown Business, 2003.

CHAPTER 4 CONVERT YOUR IDEA INTO A PROJECT

Bungay Stanier, Michael. *Do More Great Work: Stop the Busywork, and Start the Work That Matters*. New York: Workman, 2010.

Duhigg, Charles. *Smarter Faster Better: The Transformative Power of Real Productivity*. New York: Random House, 2016.

Dweck, Carol. *Mindset: The New Psychology of Success*. New York: Ballantine, 2007.

McChesney, Chris, Sean Covey, and Jim Huling. *The 4 Disciplines of Execution: Achieving Your Wildly Important Goals*. New York: Free Press, 2016.

Mohr, Tara Sophia. *Playing Big: Practical Wisdom for Women Who Want to Speak Up, Create, and Lead*. New York: Avery, 2015.

CHAPTER 5 MAKE SPACE FOR YOUR PROJECT

Loehr, Jim, and Tony Schwartz. *The Power of Full Engagement: Managing Energy, Not Time, Is the Key to High Performance and Personal Renewal*. New York: Free Press, 2003.

Moran, Brian P., and Michael Lennington. *The 12 Week Year: Get More Done in 12 Weeks Than Others Do in 12 Months*. Hoboken, NJ: Wiley, 2013.

Newport, Cal. *Deep Work: Rules for Focused Success in a Distracted World*. New York: Grand Central, 2016.

Sutherland, Jeff, and J. J. Sutherland. *Scrum: The Art of Doing Twice the Work in Half the Time*. New York: Currency, 2014.

CHAPTER 6   BUILD YOUR PROJECT ROAD MAP

Gallup and Tom Rath. *StrengthsFinder2.0*. Washington, DC: Gallup Press, 2007.

Knapp, Jake, with John Zeratsky, and Braden Kowitz. *Sprint: How to Solve Big Problems and Test New Ideas in Just Five Days*. New York: Simon and Schuster, 2016.

Mecham, Jesse. *You Need a Budget: The Proven System for Breaking the Paycheck-to-Paycheck Cycle, Getting Out of Debt, and Living the Life You Want*. New York: Harper Business, 2017.

Timmons, Jacquette M. *Financial Intimacy: How to Create a Healthy Relationship with Your Money and Your Mate*. Chicago: Chicago Review Press, 2009.

CHAPTER 7   KEEP FLYING BY ACCOUNTING FOR DRAG POINTS

Kashdan, Todd, and Robert Biswas-Diener. *The Upside of Your Dark Side: Why Being Your Whole Self—Not Just Your "Good" Self—Drives Success and Fulfillment*. New York: Plume, 2015.

Scott, Susan. *Fierce Conversations: Achieving Success at Work and in Life, One Conversation at a Time*. New York: Berkley Books, 2004.

Sutton, Robert I. *The No Asshole Rule: Building a Civilized Workplace and Surviving One That Isn't*. New York: Business Plus, 2010.

Ury, William. *The Power of a Positive No: Save the Deal, Save the Relationship—and Still Say No*. New York: Bantam, 2007.

CHAPTER 8   WEAVE YOUR PROJECT INTO YOUR SCHEDULE

Becker, Joshua. *The Minimalist Home: A Room-by-Room Guide to a Decluttered, Refocused Life*. New York: WaterBrook, 2018.

Covey, Stephen R., A. Roger Merrill, and Rebecca R. Merrill. *First Things First*. New York: Free Press, 1996.

Pink, Daniel H. *When: The Scientific Secrets of Perfect Timing*. New York: Riverhead Books, 2018.

Vardy, Mike. *The Front Nine: How to Start the Year You Want Anytime You Want*. New York: Diversion Books, 2012.

CHAPTER 9   BUILD DAILY MOMENTUM

Allen, David. *Getting Things Done: The Art of Stress-Free Productivity*. New York: Penguin, 2015.

Clear, James. *Atomic Habits: An Easy and Proven Way to Build Good Habits and Break Bad Ones*. New York: Avery, 2018.

Kleon, Austin. *Show Your Work: 10 Ways to Share Your Creativity and Get Discovered*. New York: Workman, 2014.

Pressfield, Steven. *The War of Art: Break Through the Blocks and Win Your Inner Creative Battles*. Self-published, 2012.

Rao, Srinivas. *An Audience of One: Reclaiming Creativity for Its Own Sake*. New York: Portfolio, 2018.

Tracy, Brian. *Eat That Frog! 21 Ways to Stop Procrastinating and Get More Done in Less Time*. 3rd ed. Oakland, CA: Berrett-Koehler, 2017.

CHAPTER 10   FINISH STRONG

Christensen, Clayton M., James Allworth, and Karen Dillon. *How Will You Measure Your Life?* New York: Harper Business, 2012.

Heath, Chip, and Dan Heath. *The Power of Moments: Why Certain Experiences Have Extraordinary Impact*. New York: Simon and Schuster, 2017.

Slim, Pamela. *Body of Work: Finding the Thread That Ties Your Story Together*. New York: Portfolio, 2013.

ABOUT THE AUTHOR

Charlie Gilkey is an author, podcaster, teacher, speaker, and entrepreneur. He's the founder of Productive Flourishing, a web-based company that is often included in the top websites for productivity, time management, and personal development for creative people. The tools found at Productive Flourishing, including the Momentum Planners, have been downloaded and used by millions of people.

Charlie is also a PhD candidate in philosophy and a veteran of Operation Iraqi Freedom, where he served as an Army logistics officer. His background as a soldier and philosopher colors his work.

In addition to his work at Productive Flourishing, Charlie serves on the board of directors of the Wayfinding Academy and the Portland chapter of Social Venture Partners. His focus in the nonprofit community is on creating solutions that address economic, educational, and racial injustice.

He lives with his wife in Portland, Oregon. For more, visit ProductiveFlourishing.com or follow @CharlieGilkey on Twitter.

ABOUT SOUNDS TRUE

Sounds True is a multimedia publisher whose mission is to inspire and support personal transformation and spiritual awakening. Founded in 1985 and located in Boulder, Colorado, we work with many of the leading spiritual teachers, thinkers, healers, and visionary artists of our time. We strive with every title to preserve the essential "living wisdom" of the author or artist. It is our goal to create products that not only provide information to a reader or listener, but that also embody the quality of a wisdom transmission.

For those seeking genuine transformation, Sounds True is your trusted partner. At SoundsTrue.com you will find a wealth of free resources to support your journey, including exclusive weekly audio interviews, free downloads, interactive learning tools, and other special savings on all our titles.

To learn more, please visit SoundsTrue.com/freegifts or call us toll-free at 800.333.9185.